FOR SALE BY OWNER
Sell your own home and save thousands

Edward M. Walsh, LL.B.

Self-Counsel Press
(a division of)
International Self-Counsel Press Ltd.
Canada   U.S.A.

Printed in Canada

First edition: June, 1980
Second edition: May, 1984
Third edition: March, 1987; Reprinted: November, 1988; January, 1990
Fourth edition: January, 1992; Reprinted: November, 1992
Fifth edition: September, 1994

Canadian Cataloguing in Publication Data

Walsh, Edward M. (Edward Michael), 1941-
  For sale by owner

(Self-counsel legal series)
Previous ed. by Russell Oddy.
ISBN 0-88908-519-6

  1. House selling — Canada.   I. Oddy, Russell, 1916-
II. Title.   III. Series.
HD1379.032   1994   333.33'8   C94-910564-3

Cover photo by Terry Guscott, ATN Visuals, Vancouver, B.C.

Models supplied by Blanche's Model and Talent Management, Vancouver, B.C.

Self-Counsel Press
(a division of)
International Self-Counsel Press Ltd.

Head and Editorial Office	*U.S. Address*
1481 Charlotte Road	1704 N. State Street
North Vancouver, B.C. V7J lHl	Bellingham, WA 98225

CONTENTS

iii

TABLES

SAMPLES

If, after reading this book, you wish to draw up your own agreement of purchase and sale, Self-Counsel Press has available the appropriate forms for British Columbia and Ontario. Use the order form below.

ORDER FORM

- -

To: Self-Counsel Press
1481 Charlotte Road
North Vancouver, B.C.
V7J 1H1

Self-Counsel Press
8-2283 Argentia Road
Mississauga, Ontario
L5N 5Z2

Please send me —

_____sets of "Interim Agreement" for British Columbia (includes three copies).

_____sets of "Agreement of Purchase and Sale" for Ontario (includes three copies)

Each set costs $3.95. Please add $2.50 postage and handling, plus G.S.T. and P.S.T. Prices subject to change without notice.

Name: _____

Address: _____

City: _____Province: _____

Postal code: _____Telephone number: _____

Please charge to my ❑ Visa ❑ MasterCard

MasterCard/Visa number: _____

Expiry date: _____Signature: _____

(Please allow three to four weeks delivery.)

NOTICE TO READERS

INTRODUCTION

It is no wonder so many people want to sell their homes by themselves, instead of using a sales agent. Have you calculated real estate commission fees and taxes lately? They range as high as 6% and sometimes 7% of your sale price. During the seventies and eighties, homes jumped in value. A home selling for $75 000 fifteen years ago could easily be selling for $325 000 in today's market. In that short space of time the commission fee rose from $4 500 to $19 500 on a six percent rate. Add the Goods and Services Tax (GST) to your marketing costs and it's a staggering $20 865. An average home selling for $170 000 will cost you over $10 000 in real estate commission based on the same rate.

Selling privately is easy and inexpensive when you know how. Before real estate agents, many of our great grandparents sold privately with the assistance of a lawyer, yet the average owner today is reluctant to attempt it on his or her own. There may be many reasons why, but I hope negative reports cautioning against a do-it-yourself approach isn't one of them. I'm not suggesting a private sale by owner is for everyone, but if you have time, patience, and a modest budget, the financial rewards are worth it. It's easy; most homes sell themselves. All you need is a tried and true method as revealed in this step-by-step guide.

Your journey begins by completing a few preliminaries, gathering the relevant data, ascertaining your financing options, and choosing the right lawyer. After looking into the availability of a future accommodation, follow my suggestions for setting a selling price. The step-by-step procedure is informative for all vendors — even those who may later decide to use an agent. By informing yourself, you don't have to rely exclusively on an agent.

Consider your savings: no real estate commission fee and no GST! Put into action the simple procedural advertising guides, wait for the enquiries, and then apply the five simple selling strategies to your "hot prospects," who are then ready to sign on the dotted line. Wait for expiry of the conditional period, get the waiver form signed, and you're virtually home free. Last, finalize your new living accommodation and leave the rest up to your lawyer; it's that simple.

My book shows you how to deal with real estate agents, especially those of lesser professional integrity; they'll use every tactic in the book to weaken your enthusiasm. Professional real estate agents perform an excellent service — but so can you. Think of the thousands of dollars you can save, including the GST. Have fun learning about a fascinating business. Good luck. I know you can do it.

1

ATTEND TO THE PRELIMINARIES

Selling your home privately can be exciting, time-consuming, agonizing, and very rewarding. You could put thousands of dollars in your pocket while enjoying a competitive price advantage over the rest of the market. You don't have to depend on luck if you use the correct selling strategies.

To obtain the selling results you want, you need a plan. But even the best-laid plans are futile without appropriate preliminary action. When you apply for a job interview, you must prepare by dressing properly and researching the company; when you plan to sell your own home, you first need to tend to the tasks outlined below.

a. CONDUCT A MAINTENANCE EXAMINATION

Used car dealers take in cars on trade. The cars are examined, cleaned, and minor repairs are made. Almost daily they are washed down to look fresh and clean. This is the approach you should take with your home and premises. Imagine yourself peering at your home and property with the eye of a critical, prudent, and knowledgeable purchaser. Distance yourself from your personal attachment. Try to envision the home as an investment for sale purposes. Ask yourself, "Can I objectively examine the property critically and make the cosmetic changes needed to show its best appearance?"

Consult a knowledgeable friend experienced in real estate. His or her honest opinion is invaluable. Determine if there are any objections regarding curb appeal, landscaping, furniture layout, wall covering, and overall condition. Invite

1

criticism and suggestions; sometimes we forget about junk accumulating in the garage or basement. It is amazing how small things can make a big difference. Adding a few shrubs and colorful plants can dress up a lackluster curb appeal. Examine brick work, stucco, and siding, and have minor repairs completed. Use a ladder to physically examine the roof, eaves trough, upper chimney bricks, flashings, and any other potential problem areas. Experience proves that money and time spent now provides tenfold returns in the future.

Are the grounds clean, well-groomed, and manicured? Fencing, sheds, cars, machinery, and other objects which are dilapidated and run down create an undesirable environment. Rooms and closets should be free from clutter. Too much furniture in one room looks crowded and makes an averaged-sized room look too small. Change dark wall coverings and dark paint to lighter shades unless they are part of a professional interior decorating design. Pastels and neutral colors complement most furniture and provide a bright, fresh, and airy atmosphere. Have you noticed that real estate agents always turn on artificial lights before a showing? Place extra lamps in those areas where natural light is limited. Walls, flooring, windows, and light fixtures must be sparkling clean. Animal smells, smoke residue, mold, and dust are offensive and turn purchasers away. A fresh light scent emitting from the carpet will have a positive psychological effect on the purchaser. See the pre-sale maintenance guidelines shown in Sample #1.

b. DECIDE IF MORE TIME AND MONEY SHOULD BE INVESTED

Determine if a major expenditure should be undertaken before exposing the property to the market. For example, fuel bills may be excessive and the furnace may be on its last legs. Perhaps the roof shingles are curled, revealing major deterioration. Maybe the foundation is cracked, allowing water to seep into the basement. Is it economically sound to pour more

SAMPLE #1
PRE-SALE MAINTENANCE GUIDELINES

AREA	WORK DETAILS*	TIME	$COST
EXTERIOR			

1. Exterior grounds

debris & weeds
shrubs
flower-beds
shed
fences

2. Exterior home

wood
stone
brick
stucco
aluminum
vinyl
windows
eaves trough
roof

3. Front entrance

steps
porch
door
mail box
brass-work
screen
door bell

4. Rear entrance

steps
door
door bell
screen

5. Garage

doors
window
opener

NOTE: *Complete work details with either (a) acceptable, (b) clean, (c) paint, (d) re-arrange, (e) service, (f) repair or (g) replace.*

siding
roof

INTERIOR HOME

1. Front hall

door
window
light fixture
flooring
closet
decor
other

2. Rear hall

door
window
ceiling
walls
light fixture
flooring
closet
decor
other

3. Kitchen

doors
windows
ceiling
walls
light fixtures
cupboards
pantry
sink(s)
plumbing
flooring
decor
other

4. Dining room

doors
windows
ceiling

walls
light fixture
flooring
decor
other

5. **Living room**

doors
windows
ceiling
walls
light fixture
flooring
decor
other

6. **Family room**

doors
windows
ceiling
walls
light fixtures
flooring
decor
other

7. **Powder room**

door
window
ceiling
light fixtures
toilet
sink
plumbing
flooring
decor
other

8. **Bathroom**

doors
windows
ceiling
walls

    light fixtures
    bath
    shower
    tiles
    toilet
    sink(s)
    plumbing
    flooring
    decor
    other

9. **Master bedroom**

    doors
    windows
    ceiling
    walls
    light fixtures
    closets
    flooring
    decor
    other

10. **En-suite bathroom**

    door
    window
    ceiling
    walls
    light fixtures
    bath
    shower
    toilet
    sink(s)
    plumbing
    tile
    flooring
    decor
    other

11. **Other bedroom**

    doors
    windows
    ceiling
    walls

light fixtures
closets
flooring
decor
other

12. Main stairs

doors
windows
ceiling
walls
light fixtures
flooring
decor
other

13. Basement stairs

doors
windows
ceiling
walls
light fixtures
flooring
decor
other

14. Recreational room

doors
windows
ceiling
walls
light fixtures
flooring
decor
other

15. Basement

doors
windows
walls
ceiling
flooring
light fixtures

storage
cold room
decor
other

FUNCTIONAL SYSTEMS

1. **Fireplace**

   chamber
   chimney

2. **Furnace**

   filter
   electronic cleaner
   fan

3. **Electrical**

   service panel
   wiring
   receptacles

4. **Plumbing**

   piping lines
   fixtures
   taps

5. **Air conditioning**

   filter
   fan
   fluid

6. **Hot water tank**

   capacity
   type
   source

7. **Insulation**

   ceiling
   basement walls

8. **Other**

money into your property? Can the additional costs be recouped by increasing the selling price, or have you lost your competitive advantage?

Ask yourself, "Will leaving the repair or replacement undone turn off potential purchasers?" In each situation, weigh the cost, the availability of money, and the problem's possible negative effect on interested buyers. Remember that purchasers employ the principle of substitution: they won't pay more for your property than the cost of acquiring an equally desirable substitute on the open market. Assume that there is an adequate inventory of homes on the market.

Obtain quotes from at least two reputable contractors in the trade. You may find the job isn't major after all. At any rate, written quotations provide excellent material for putting purchasers at ease and to counter exaggerated objections. The ultimate decision is yours, so don't let a deal turn on this issue alone.

c. DECIDE IF THE SERVICES OF A PROFESSIONAL ARE NEEDED

This is a personal decision. The cost may be worth it, especially if you feel uneasy or uncomfortable about conducting your own examination. Most people have limited knowledge about building construction, its mechanical equipment, and the component materials. Experienced home inspectors provide that type of assistance. They provide written reports about the condition and life expectancy of component parts such as the roof, furnace, and air conditioning. It is an independent report to assist you in examining and determining recommended repairs and overall condition. (Beware of using inspectors who recommend particular tradespeople to do the job).

Today anyone can call themselves a home inspector because the formal requirements are almost nonexistent. Home inspectors should have extensive knowledge and experience in building construction through involvement in the home renovation industry, residential construction, or as building inspectors who were employed in the municipal building department. Ascertain if the person is a member of the American Society of Home Inspectors (ASHI). To my knowledge, the only regulatory body affecting home inspectors in Canada is voluntary registration as a certified member of the American Society of Home Inspectors (ASHI). Local chapters are springing up in some of the provinces. Inspectors may register with either a local chapter or directly with the American society.

To qualify as a certified member and to advertise affiliation, each inspector must complete at least 250 inspections, pass two examinations, and agree to comply with the society's standards of practice and prescribed code of ethics.

As a pre-requisite for annual renewal of membership each member must establish a minimum of 20 educational credits to show that he or she has kept current with the changes in the building industry.

The home inspector's written reports are useful as a selling tool because potential purchasers will feel more confident if they can rely on a detailed report prepared by a professional. Sample #2 covers the areas you may want a home inspector to investigate.

d. EXAMINE YOUR FINANCING AND EXISTING INTEREST RATES

Financing is often forgotten until it's too late. The thousands of dollars you thought were going in your pocket could end up in the mortgage lender's pocket instead. Don't enter into negotiations to sell without first obtaining the mortgage particulars. How much is the mortgage lender going to charge as a penalty for the privilege of an early pay-out? What options do you have and what are the associated costs? Is your financing portable? What are the legal and administrative costs? Will there be an interest differential? Can the

SAMPLE #2
HOME INSPECTOR REPORT CHECKLIST

FOUNDATION AND FOOTING	Yes	No	Unknown
1. Is the home constructed on solid earth?	____	____	____
2. Is the ground sloped away from the foundation?	____	____	____
3. Are the footings below the frost line?	____	____	____
4. Is there good floor drainage?	____	____	____
5. Is there a working sump pump?	____	____	____
6. Does the basement appear to be dry year round with no evidence of water problems?	____	____	____
7. Is the sill plate firmly attached to the top of the foundation?	____	____	____
8. Is there adequate ventilation in the basement or crawl space?	____	____	____
9. Are the walls of the foundation free of major cracks, deterioration and settling?	____	____	____
10. Is there adequate insulation on the interior or exterior foundation walls?	____	____	____

FRAMING CHECKLIST

	Yes	No	Unknown
1. Is there adequate insulation and protection provided continuously between the house sill plate and foundation?	____	____	____
2. Are the floor joints structurally sound and not subject to sagging, bowing or springiness?	____	____	____
3. Are the floors quiet and solid when walked upon?	____	____	____

4. Are the walls structurally sound? ____ ____ ____

5. Are all load bearing beams structurally sound and not deteriorated by rot or, in the case of metal, evidence of excessive rust? ____ ____ ____

6. Is there adequate bracing to restrain joists from twisting? ____ ____ ____

7. Is there adequate insulation in the walls? ____ ____ ____

8. Is there adequate insulation in the ceiling? ____ ____ ____

9. Is there evidence of wall or ceiling mold or condensation? ____ ____ ____

10. Are lintel loads over openings structurally sound? ____ ____ ____

11. Are the roof lines straight with no evidence of sagging? ____ ____ ____

12. Are roof rafters or trusses free of rot, termite, or fire damage? ____ ____ ____

13. Are roof rafters or trusses properly spanned and spaced apart with no sagging or buckling? ____ ____ ____

14. Does the attic have proper ventilation with no visible condensation problems? ____ ____ ____

15. Are the collar ties and bracing in the roof adequately secured? ____ ____ ____

16. Is the roof sheathing properly secured with no swelling or de-lamination? ____ ____ ____

17. Is there any evidence of rot? ____ ____ ____

ELECTRICAL SYSTEM

1. Is copper wiring used throughout? ___ ___ ___

2. Does the house have a minimum 240-volt power supply? ___ ___ ___

3. Is there a minimum of two 100-amp. fuses in the main disconnect? ___ ___ ___

4. Is the copper wiring minimum #14 gauge to carry 15 amps.? ___ ___ ___

5. Is the service panel supplied with circuit breakers as opposed to fuses? ___ ___ ___

6. Is there enough power for the normal appliances and the electrical components usually operated in a household? ___ ___ ___

7. Are there enough separate circuits? ___ ___ ___

8. Are the standard receptacles throughout the house three hole grounded outlets? ___ ___ ___

9. Does the bathroom have a ground fault interrupt or safety receptacles to safeguard against accidental electrocution if contact is made with sink or other water? ___ ___ ___

10. Are there sufficient enough receptacles in all rooms including the basement, garage, and attic? ___ ___ ___

HEATING AND COOLING

1. Is the heating unit adequately sized to generate sufficient heat and distribute it to all areas of the home? ___ ___ ___

2. Is the heating system economical? ___ ___ ___

3. Is the heating system excessively noisy when in operation? ___ ___ ___

4. Is the cooling unit adequately sized to cool all areas of the home efficiently? ___ ___ ___

5. Is the cooling system excessively noisy when in operation? ___ ___ ___

FIREPLACE AND CHIMNEY

1. Does the fireplace work properly with adequate draw? ___ ___ ___

2. Is the chimney flue area at least one-twelfth the size of the fireplace opening? ___ ___ ___

3. Is the fireplace properly constructed or installed? ___ ___ ___

4. Has the chimney and fireplace been cleaned annually? ___ ___ ___

WOOD STOVES

1. Does the wood-stove have adequate clearance from combustible materials? ___ ___ ___

2. Does the exhaust flue and chimney system have good connections? ___ ___ ___

3. Is there excessive creosote deposit in the chimney? ___ ___ ___

PLUMBING

1. Is the water supplied at a sufficiently high pressure? ___ ___ ___

2. Is the interior piping composed
   of copper?   ____ ____ ____

3. Is there a main water shut off
   valve where the supply of water
   enters the house?   ____ ____ ____

4. Is the plumbing noisy when the
   water is engaged under pressure? ____ ____ ____

5. Are all plumbing fixtures
   properly vented?   ____ ____ ____

6. If septic tank is used, has it been
   cleaned recently?   ____ ____ ____

7. Is the house free from natural
   gas odors?   ____ ____ ____

8. Do the toilets have a powerful
   enough flushing action?   ____ ____ ____

HOT WATER HEATERS

1. Is the water heater less than
   five years old?   ____ ____ ____

2. Does the tank appear to be in
   good condition?   ____ ____ ____

3. When the overflow valve is
   engaged, does rusty water
   discontinue and become clear? ____ ____ ____

4. Is the temperature dial turned to
   a moderate setting?   ____ ____ ____

EXTERIOR WALL FINISHES

1. Does the wall finish require little
   maintenance?   ____ ____ ____

2. Is the wall finish in good
   condition?   ____ ____ ____

3. Have all joint seams been properly sealed with caulking or flashing? ____ ____ ____

4. Does the wall finish have more than 25% life expectancy? ____ ____ ____

5. Is any buckling or bowing evident in the material? ____ ____ ____

6. Do painted areas show blistering or peeling? ____ ____ ____

WINDOWS

1. Do all windows operate correctly? ____ ____ ____

2. Do the windows show excessive water stains? ____ ____ ____

3. Are the panes between the glazing free of condensation causing no discoloration? ____ ____ ____

4. Are the window frames caulked properly outside? ____ ____ ____

5. Are the windows at least double glazing? ____ ____ ____

6. Is the double glazing factory sealed and designed to have no air infiltration or ex-filtration between the panes of glass? ____ ____ ____

EXTERIOR DOORS

1. Are all exterior doors made of solid wood or insulated steel? ____ ____ ____

2. Are all doors latched securely and weather-tight? ____ ____ ____

3. Are all door frames properly caulked? ____ ____ ____

ROOFS

1. Does the roof have at least ten years life expectancy before major repair or replacement? ____ ____ ____

2. Does the roof appear to be waterproof with no loose, missing, or repaired shingles and no signs of inside water damage? ____ ____ ____

3. Is all flashing properly installed and in good condition? ____ ____ ____

PRIVATE WELLS

1. Has the water been tested to determine suitability for drinking? ____ ____ ____

2. Does the well have sufficient capacity at all times of the year? ____ ____ ____

3. Does the water system provide adequate pressure? ____ ____ ____

4. Does the water system have a safety shutoff valve? ____ ____ ____

purchaser assume your mortgage and if so, what are the conditions? How and when do you get a release of personal liability? Is there an advantage comparing interest rates on your mortgage compared to current rates? What are the current mortgage rates for one to five year terms? Is the interest rate for those terms different if the mortgage is conventional or insured?

Seek the answers to these questions in order to negotiate in your best interest with both the mortgage lender and the purchaser. It is impossible to employ the best selling strategies without having those answers. Set up an interest rate journal. On a weekly basis, preferably Fridays, contact your conventional lender to obtain the current interest rates on conventional mortgages for terms ranging from one to five years. If the interest rates are different for insured mortgages, record those rates separately. Later we will discuss how this information can usefully be employed to assist you in selling your home. The method for obtaining your mortgage particulars is discussed in chapter 2.

e. DETERMINE THE EARLIEST DATE YOU CAN COMPLETE THE SALE

Determining in advance the earliest date you can complete your sale is important for the purchaser. Suppose you have someone interested who sold their property with a 60-day closing date. It means they have to be out on that date. You will be hard pressed to convince those purchasers to sign an agreement for a later closing date. Have you considered an alternative accommodation in the event of a sale? In order to sell quickly you need to consider the availability of another place to live, especially if the purchaser is under pressure to move within a time frame. Finding other accommodation is discussed in chapter 12. As a rule of thumb, attempt to arrange your affairs so you can close your deal within 60 days to accommodate most purchasers.

18

f. LOCATE ALL LEGAL DOCUMENTS

Collect your legal papers such as the deed or transfer document, the lawyer's reporting letter that was forwarded to you when you purchased your home, the survey, the agreements with others affecting the property, and the mortgage papers. Later you will learn how these documents are needed for completing part of the agreement of purchase and sale. If any of the legal terms used in real estate transactions are unfamiliar to you, check the Glossary at the end of the book.

g. CREATE A SELLING ATMOSPHERE

Having chosen to sell privately, you have to wear two hats. As the seller, you're known as the vendor, and as the person selling, you're the salesperson.

Being the vendor, you must keep the property in an immaculate state for showing; it is a lot of work, but it is worth the effort. Keep a good supply of air fresheners on hand, especially with animals and habitual smokers. Your living habits are your own business, but if you expect to get the top price, then you must create a pleasing atmosphere.

Doctors' homes sell faster. The appeal of associating with people who are successful should not be underestimated. As a salesperson, appear professional and successful. Always be pleasant, co-operative, and accommodating in your dealings with people contacting you about your property, even those who initially appear uninterested.

Decide whether you or your partner should play this role; for example, who is least likely to argue with those considering your property? Purchasers often require additional information, and regardless of its triviality, you must be co-operative and truthful. Evasiveness or an "I don't know" attitude gives the impression you have something to hide or you're not willing to assist. There is no such thing as a perfect home, so don't try to avoid addressing valid objections. Your honesty and co-operation wins the confidence and approval of the purchaser, a necessary ingredient for a successful sale.

Now that you have considered or completed the preliminaries, your next step is to prepare a property particulars statement, as discussed in the next chapter.

2

YOUR PROPERTY PARTICULARS STATEMENT

The property particulars statement provides the relevant facts you need for implementing your sales program, and it is a source of information for preparing the agreement of purchase and sale. You are selling something you own, but you'll still need to do research.

Most of us have sold articles at one time or another, such as a bicycle, a car, a boat, or a piece of furniture. After the preliminaries of cleaning and getting the sale item into shape, you assemble the important facts for describing it, advertising it, and selling it.

For a car, you make a list of its features, such as the manufacturer's name, the year and model, the engine size, the horse power, and any options, features, or equipment before you advertise and sell it. A similar process is involved with selling your home.

The information you assemble now will be used later in your advertising program, your sales pitch, and for preparing the sales agreement. The steps you need to take are discussed below.

a. PROPERTY DESCRIPTION AND RESTRICTIONS

For selling purposes, property description is chiefly concerned with the legal description, not the municipal address. For legally determining the location and land dimensions of your property, you need the full legal description as shown in the ownership document.

Property restrictions are often attached to legal descriptions. For example, a right of way permitting others to travel over your property is a restriction. Building schemes in new subdivisions often have restrictions. Such schemes list a variety of activities that are prohibited. For example, you may be prevented from parking recreational vehicles on your driveway, or you may be prohibited from erecting fencing over four feet in height.

Rights enjoyed by neighbors or others over your property and prohibited activities against using your property are restrictions. To properly identify the extent of your property title, you need to know about any restrictions. A restriction must be written into your sales agreement if you expect purchasers to accept it.

Suppose for example, you examined two identical cars side by side, and the capacity of one of the cars to reach its top performance is restricted because of an inadequately-sized engine. The car's restriction is not observable without an engineered test. Similarly, the property restrictions go undetected by purchasers buying a home. The purchaser's lawyer conducts a title search to determine, among other things, if restrictions are attached to your property that aren't mentioned in the agreement of purchase and sale. When you fail to write property restrictions into the agreement, an opportunity exists for the purchaser to cancel the deal. To prevent this from happening, you must include all property restrictions in the sales agreement to legally bind purchasers.

You can find out about restrictions registered against your property without paying the cost of another title search. The reporting letter your lawyer gave you after you purchased your property should show if restrictions exist. When the reporting letter gives no indication, contact your lawyer for a review of your file to determine if any property restrictions were discovered when the title search was done. Sample #3 shows a property verification form for obtaining this information.

b. IMPROVEMENTS

Improvements are features enhancing your property's value. Examples of improvements are swimming pools, exceptional landscaping, a coach house with a bachelor's apartment, or anything unique or special which is not normally found in similar properties. List each improvement showing the particular benefits of having it and any outstanding features.

c. ASSESSMENT OF SPECULATIVE VALUE

A residential home sometimes has speculative value. Suppose you own a large, two-storey heritage home located in the heart of town surrounded by older, mature homes with a mix of residential, medical, and legal uses. If the recorded zoning at city hall allows mixed uses, it means you are legally permitted to use the property for other uses. When the home is easily adaptable to another use, such as offices, your property may be more valuable to an investor than a residential home buyer. Ask at the city hall building department to determine if your property has this kind of potential speculative value. City hall officials are available to give advice on zoning uses and the future development plans intended for your property and the surrounding area.

Sometimes a property has an extra-wide frontage making it possible to obtain approval to sever off one or more building lots. The ability to sever gives you potential speculative value attractive to small builders.

Therefore, if your property's land size or zoning creates a potential speculative opportunity, explore the possibilities and later you can target those who might have a greater interest in buying your property than residential purchasers.

199–____

To_____
(lawyer)

_____
(address)

Re: property_____
(address of property for sale)

You acted on my behalf when I purchased the above property.

Presently, I am in the process of selling my home. Please provide me with the following information from the search notes and my file:

1. The full legal description of my property: _____

_____

2. Particulars of restrictions, limitations, or easements disclosed by the search notes: _____

_____

3. Any further information the search notes disclose relevant to a sale of my property: _____

_____

This information is needed by me to properly complete the agreement of purchase and sale form with a future purchaser.

_____
(owner)

N.B. I enclose a stamped, self-addressed envelope for the return of the completed form.

---

d. EXTERNAL AND INTERNAL FEATURES

Record details of the external and internal features of your home and ensure your calculations are accurate. In determining your home's square footage, measure the outside perimeter walls for the main level, and the inside perimeter walls for the upper level, but add the thickness for upper walls. Be accurate and consistent in recording your measurements. Each interior room should be measured from the inside walls. Physically record the particulars of each room, noting floor measurements, window sizes, flooring type, and other special features.

Electrical, plumbing, heating, cooling, and insulation systems require some expertise. You might find it worth consulting a private home inspector, local building official, or friend knowledgeable in the building industry to itemize and correctly describe each system's specifications.

e. LIST DISTANCES TO ESSENTIAL SERVICES AND AMENITIES

Calculate the distances from your home to essential services and amenities. Families with young children and teenagers want easy access to schools and colleges. Older, retired couples want easy access to ambulance, hospital, fire, and police services. Every buyer has different priorities. Make a list of distances to each essential service. How far are the religious, recreational, cultural, and shopping facilities? Information that shows your home's proximity to services and facilities is worth including if it helps potential purchasers choose your property over the competition.

f. LIST HOME OWNERSHIP EXPENSES

Calculate and list your home ownership expenses. How much are the municipal taxes? What are the total electricity, heating, and water charges? Huge differences sometimes exist between the costs associated with your home as compared with other homes on the market. Consumption varies from home owner to home owner, but it is information purchasers need in order to make a decision.

g. CONDUCT A NEIGHBORHOOD ANALYSIS

A neighborhood may have a unique attraction for some homogeneous groups. Is there an ethnic, religious, cultural, age, or occupational group interested in your neighborhood? Does your neighborhood attract one of those particular groups? This information helps you to target those groups later in your advertising program.

h. OBTAIN YOUR MORTGAGE PARTICULARS

The easiest way to obtain your mortgage particulars is to send your mortgage lender a mortgage verification form (see Sample #4). The mortgage verification form tells lenders you are selling and requests information about the mortgage amount, interest rate, monthly payment, expiry date, penalties, privileges, options and other features. The mortgage lender fills in the information needed, and returns it to you in your self-addressed, stamped envelope. Read the next chapter to see how mortgage particulars are used to assess your financing options.

i. ASSESS YOUR COMPETITION

Determine your competition in the marketplace. Drive around and record addresses and phone numbers of properties for sale that are similar to yours. Contact each home owner or real estate agent by phone to get as much information as possible about the property advertised for sale. For example, you need to know —

(a) the selling price,

(b) the lot dimensions,

(c) the building size and type,

SAMPLE #4
MORTGAGE VERIFICATION FORM

_____19____

To_____
        (name of mortgage company)

_____
    (address)

     Re: Mortgage no._____

_____   _____
     (print owner's name)   *(signature)*

_____
     (address)

The above mortgage is held by you. Presently, I am in the process of selling my property and I need the following information:

Type of mortgage   _____
     (conventional or insured)

Principal balance outstanding $_____ as of _____ 19_____

Amortization period _____ Due date _____ 19_____

Annual prepayment privilege _____ Amount $_____
     (yes or no)

Other prepayment privileges _____

May this mortgage be paid out in full? _____
Pay-out penalty $_____   *(yes or no)*
Is this mortgage portable _____
     (yes or no)

Is this mortgage assumable?_____
     (yes or no)

Does the purchaser need approval to assume? _____
     (yes or no)

If purchaser is approved to assume am I released from further liability on this mortgage? _____
     (yes or no)

_____
     Mortgagee

N.B. *I enclose a stamped, self-addressed envelope for the return of the completed form.*

(d) the general condition of the property,

(e) any special features, and

(f) the approximate length of time the property has been on the market.

Make a personal inspection of each home to complete the list of particulars noted above. Obtain information on at least a minimum of four or five similar properties. After the inspection, record your comments in a journal with objective reasons why that property is either superior or inferior to your property. Later, the information can be used in a variety of ways, such as making property comparisons in your selling pitch to potential purchasers, and as a guide for setting your selling price. In chapter 6, a method is suggested for setting your selling price to gain an advantage over the competition.

By carefully identifying, examining, and recording relevant facts, you have at your fingertips information needed at all stages of the selling process. The foundation of knowledge for selling starts with this document. It's a reference you'll use over and over for preparing advertising and selling strategies. Sample #5 shows a property particulars statement. You can use it as a guide to assist you in gathering relevant facts about your home and other homes in your neighborhood. The more you know about your home, the likelier you are to succeed at selling your home privately.

PROPERTY PARTICULARS STATEMENT

Municipal address _____

Legal owners _____

_____

Name of party(s) who have interest in my property

_____

LAND CHARACTERISTICS

Legal description of land to be shown on offer to purchase (as shown in ownership document or property verification form)

Restrictions or limitations to land (as shown in the lawyer's reporting letter or the property verification form)

    (a)   mutual right of way

    (b)   other easements

    (c)   building restrictions

    (d)   restrictive covenants

    (e)   licence agreements

Dimensions of land _____ _____ shape of land_____

Soil type _____ condition _____

Zoning provisions _____

Official plan provisions _____

Are land dimensions large enough for an addition to the home?
rear yard _____ side yard _____ front yard _____

Is side yard large enough for separate building lot(s)? _____

Is land large enough for small subdivision or condominium project?

_____

Municipal assessment value $ _____
Annual taxes $_____

Local improvements or special assessments $_____

Who are adjoining owners (re: privacy)? Residential _____,

Commercial _____ Institutional _____ Industrial _____,

Governmental _____

IMPROVEMENTS

Fenced yard _____

Patio _____ wood or stone _____

Swimming pool: above _____ in-ground _____ size _____

Detached garage _____ size _____

Storage shed _____ size _____

Special landscaping _____

Mature trees and shrubs _____

Driveways and walk ways type _____ asphalt _____

concrete _____ gravel _____ stone _____

Other special features _____

EXTERIOR HOME

Home facing north _____ south _____ east _____ west _____

Type, one storey_____ storey and a half_____ two storey_____

three storey/multi-storey_____

Kind of accommodation, detached_____ semi _____

town house _____ duplex _____

Exterior wall finish   brick _____ stone _____

concrete _____ block _____ stucco _____wood _____

metal _____ vinyl _____ insul brick _____asbestos _____

clay _____ slate _____ hardboard _____

Attached garage _____ no. of cars _____

Covered front porch _____

Enclosed front porch _____

Attached patio size _____   _____ wood type _____

metal _____ concrete _____ masonry _____

Type of roof asphalt _____wood_____metal_____

corrugated plastic _____built-up_____rolled_____

Recent repairs _____ date _____cost (receipts)_____

Type of eaves troughs and down spouts _____

Type of foundation poured concrete _____ concrete block_____

brick _____ stone _____ clay tile _____ cinder block _____ wood____

INTERIOR HOME

Main floor functional lay out: center hall plan_____open concept_____

Soundproofing between common walls for attached family units _____

Ceiling height_____ cathedral _____what rooms _____

skylights _____ room(s) special ceiling trim _____ room(s)

Type of windows single pane_____double pane _____

thermal pane _____Other _____

Type of trim around doors _____windows _____floor_____

Type of doors to outside insulated_____ non-insulated_____

Interior door type_____

Stairway type _____

KITCHEN

Dimensions _____ eat-in _____galley type_____

Cupboards approximate age _____style _____

type of material _____ number of lineal ft _____

Single sink _____ sink and half _____ double sink _____

garburator _____ spray hose _____

Dishwasher _____ built-in _____ portable _____

Built-in stove _____ number of burners _____ gas _____

electric _____ other _____

Food preparation island _____ size _____

Pantry _____ size _____   _____

Other built-in kitchen appliances included _____

Floor covering original _____ newer _____ type _____

Other special features _____

MAIN FLOOR LAUNDRY FACILITY

Dimensions _____

General access _____

Cupboard space _____ lineal feet _____

Floor covering _____

DINING ROOM

Dimensions _____   _____

Access to the kitchen

Floor covering _____

Special features _____

Type of chandelier _____ included _____ excluded _____

LIVING ROOM

Dimensions _____   _____

floor covering _____

Fireplace _____

Window sizes _____   _____

Special features _____

FAMILY ROOM

Dimensions _____   _____

Fireplace _____

Window sizes _____

Access to outside _____ to kitchen _____

Fireplace _____

Floor covering _____

Special features _____

STUDY OR DEN

Dimensions _____   _____

Shelving built-in _____ lineal feet _____

Floor covering _____

Special features _____

POWDER ROOM

Dimensions _____   _____

Number of plumbing fixtures _____

Floor covering _____

Special features _____

MASTER BEDROOM

Dimensions _____   _____

Floor covering

Window sizes _____   _____ window coverings included _____

Length of closet space _____

En-suite privilege _____ number of plumbing fixtures_____

Floor covering _____

Sitting area _____ size _____   _____

Fireplace _____

Access to deck _____

OTHER BEDROOMS

Dimensions _____   _____

Length of closet space _____

Window sizes _____   _____

Floor covering _____

Conversion possibilities to: Office _____ Den _____

Television room _____ recreation _____ Sewing room _____

BATHROOM(S)

Dimensions _____   _____

Fixtures: pedestal sink _____ sink and vanity _____ single sink _____

double sink _____ tub combined with shower_____

separate shower stall _____ type of material _____

Closet size _____   _____

Floor covering _____

Special features _____

ADDITIONAL CLOSETS

Location _____

Length of closet space   _____

Type _____

BASEMENT

Full _____ partial _____ percentage _____

Head room _____

Water drained by means of tile drain _____ sump pump _____ both _____

Dimensions of area completed _____   _____

Optional uses for completed area. _____

Fire place _____ wood burning stove_____

Window sizes _____   _____ number_____

Floor covering _____

Direct access to outside _____

Storage space _____ lineal feet _____

Utility area for washer and dryer _____ dimensions _____   _____

CONSTRUCTION-SYSTEMS

ELECTRICAL

Total amperage available _____ fuse panel ____ circuit breaker _____

Predominant wiring type knob-and-tube _____ rigid conduit _____

non-metallic sheathed _____ extension cord uses _____

flexible conduit _____

Type of wire used aluminum _____ copper _____

PLUMBING

Supply lines copper _____ galvanized steel _____ plastic _____

Original fixtures _____ newer _____ Approx. age _____

Water service:

municipal supply_____ community well _____ private well _____

drilled well _____ dug well _____ capacity per minute _____

water quality tested for potability_____ size of feeder line _____

Sewage municipal _____ septic tank and field bed_____

other _____

HEATING

Type unitary electrical _____ .forced air gas _____ forced air electrical _____

Boiler or hot water _____ wood or gas burning ____ gravity fed _____

other types _____

AIR CONDITIONING

Type: central _____ wall mounted _____ number of units _____

other _____

Hot water heater owned _____ rented _____

capacity_____ efficiency _____

INSULATION

Walls	type _____	thickness _____	rating _____
Ceiling	type _____	thickness_____	rating _____
Basement	type _____	thickness _____	rating _____

DISTANCE IN MILES OR KILOMETERS TO:

Municipal emergency services police _____ fire _____

ambulance _____ hospital _____

Elementary and high schools_____

Medical(doctor, dentist, etc.) _____

Shopping (grocery, pharmacy, clothing, etc.)_____

Day care _____

Public transportation _____

Major roads and highways _____

Places of worship _____

Playground _____

Parks _____

Public library_____

Exercise and sporting centers _____

Restaurants _____

Theater and the arts _____

NEIGHBORHOOD ANALYSIS

Urban _____ suburban _____ rural _____ mixed _____

Average age group

younger _____ older _____ mixed _____

Area home types

detached _____ semi _____ town house _____ mixed _____

Average age of homes

older _____ newer _____ mixed_____

Street activity

noisy and active_____ fair _____ quiet _____

Street lighting _____ sidewalks_____

General condition of surrounding homes

good _____ fair _____ poor _____

Street parking available _____ off-street parking available _____

HOME OWNERSHIP EXPENSES

Municipal taxes including local improvements and special
assessments $_____

Electrical charges (Specify if heating is included) $_____

Heating charges $_____

Water charges $ _____

Other municipal charges $_____

Cable charges $ _____

Maintenance charges $_____

Insurance charges $_____

MORTGAGE FINANCING CONSIDERATIONS

Date mortgage expires _____19_____

Amount presently outstanding on mortgage $_____

Amount of second mortgage $_____

Mortgage pay out privileges_____ pay out penalties $_____

Portability option_____

Assumption option_____

SIMILAR HOMES FOR SALE IN NEIGHBORHOOD

Number of homes for sale _____

Average price $ _____

Number for sale privately_____ number for sale by agent _____

Is your home unique _____

3

FINANCING CONSIDERATIONS

Real estate mortgaging is not like financing a motor vehicle. When you buy a car, you go to a lender, take out a loan for three to five years, make the payments, and at the end of the term you own the vehicle debt free. Mortgages involve a long-term commitment; over 95% of all home owners have mortgages. During the process of buying and selling properties, home owners must deal with mortgages. Therefore, you need to understand how to negotiate around mortgage conditions, otherwise you could lose out on an opportunity to transfer your mortgage or use it as a selling tool. Furthermore, if you aren't aware of possible penalties, you may have to pay a costly penalty that far exceeds any real estate commission fees for selling.

Imagine paying a penalty equal to the real estate agent's fee. If average homes sell for $225 000 with real estate commission fees at 6%, you're talking about $13 500. What if the mortgage penalty is $13 500 as well? Add the GST, and you're paying a staggering $27 945 for the privilege of selling your home. It's possible to get caught having to pay similar costs if you jump into a selling program without first considering your financing obligations.

Always investigate the financing before you sell. An experienced real estate agent had a sale fall through because the vendor's mortgage lender demanded $7 000 as a penalty to accept an early pay-out. The lender insisted on the full principal plus interest, a fee to provide a written signed release, plus $7 000 as a penalty to give the borrower the privilege of paying off their mortgage.

Unfortunately, the mortgage lender wasn't consulted until after an offer to buy was made by the purchaser. The vendors accepted the offer, but didn't discover liability for payment of a penalty until some time later. When asked why the mortgage particulars hadn't been obtained earlier, the agent stated there wasn't time to get those particulars between the time the listing agreement was signed and the time the offer was presented and accepted by the vendors. When the vendors eventually found out and added up all their costs, they were in the red, so they promptly refused to go through with the deal. Luckily, the purchaser hadn't firmed up the deal. Otherwise, both the vendor and the real estate agent faced a possible lawsuit.

Before implementing any sort of selling program, look into the mortgage particulars affecting your property and ask yourself the following questions:

(a) What are the mortgage terms?

(b) What type of mortgage do I have?

(c) What are the options and the privileges?

(d) How much is the penalty to pay the mortgage off?

(e) Can the mortgage be transferred to another property I am buying?

(f) Can the purchaser take over my mortgage?

(g) Is approval needed for the purchaser to assume my mortgage?

(h) Will the mortgage lender give me a release of liability when they approve the purchaser to assume my mortgage?

Examine the verification form (see Sample #4) you received from the mortgage lender. Does the form answer all the above questions? If not, go back to the lender for more information. You need the answers in order to implement your selling program, identify the financing arrangements needed by purchasers, and prepare the appropriate financing clause for your agreement of purchase and sale.

The subject of mortgaging is so extensive that entire books have been written to explain this complex subject. However, it's not necessary to understand all the complexities if you know how to avoid or minimize penalties, and if you know the ways to assist purchasers with their financing arrangements in order to select the appropriate financing clause in the agreement of purchase and sale. (See chapter 4, section **e.** for typical financing clauses.)

When you understand the importance that mortgage financing plays in the scheme of selling residential property, you'll minimize your aggravation and expense. Mortgage lenders have stacked the cards against ordinary owners selling their home. Sometimes lenders' policies actually prevent sales, so if you're planning to sell now or in the near future, find out your alternatives to protect your best interests.

a. THE THREE TYPES OF MORTGAGES

Three types of mortgages are common to residential financing. As you are selling privately, you need to understand how the different types of mortgages assist purchasers to finance your home.

1. Conventional mortgage

Most residential financing is done through conventional mortgages. Major lenders issuing this type of mortgage are restricted to lending only 75% of the value of your property. Value for mortgage purposes is always the lesser of either the selling price or the appraised value. Purchasers need at least 25% of the value of your property as a down payment to apply toward purchasing.

To illustrate, suppose you sold your home for $100 000. The maximum mortgage amount is $75 000, but to guard against collusion and inflated pricing, mortgage lenders insist on an independent estimate of value by an appraiser. If the appraisal estimate is $10 000 lower than the sale price, the maximum mortgage amount is lowered to $67 500 instead of $75 000.

That 25% the purchaser needs is called the down payment. It is always determined as a percentage of the selling price, although there are cases where the appraised value may be used if it is lower. The purchaser's down payment is a net amount because the amount actually applied towards purchasing represents the purchaser's savings after paying the anticipated costs associated with buying. For example, if the purchaser says, "I have saved $10 000 to apply toward my purchase," don't confuse this with the down payment. You have to deduct from that the associated costs of buying, such as legal fees, the appraisal fee, registration fees, taxes, etc. The purchaser's actual down payment might only be $7 000. Chapter 5 discusses the best way to get a list of the costs involved in buying a property.

2. Insured mortgage

The second type of mortgage is an insured mortgage. Major lenders issuing those types of mortgages are not restricted to the 75% rule as with conventional mortgages. Instead, lenders are permitted to lend amounts equal to 90% of the property's value. The insurer guarantees the lender that if default occurs by failure of the borrower to make payments, payment is guaranteed by the insurer. As a condition for obtaining this type of mortgage, borrowers pay a premium or fee to the insurer in addition to the normal expenses for obtaining a residential mortgage.

Presently, Canada Mortgage and Housing Corporation (CMHC) is the only insurer. The fee charged to obtain an insured mortgage is payable either up front or rolled into the mortgage amount. Although insured mortgages provide other benefits, its most important attraction for purchasers is the opportunity of paying only 10% of the property value as a down payment, instead of the 25% required for conventional mortgages.

Recently, CMHC introduced a program for first-time buyers, allowing them to apply for mortgages equal to 95% of the property value. The program permits eligible purchasers to buy with as little as five percent of the selling price and the other 95% is provided under an insured mortgage. Now with only $5 000 as a down payment, it is possible to buy a $100 000 property. The CMHC program was originally set up for two years, but has been extended because of its popularity.

CMHC reserves the right to approve lenders to issue insured mortgages and most major lenders are participants. For more information about an insured mortgage, contact either a conventional mortgage lender or the area office of CMHC.

3. High risk or equity mortgage

The third type, known as a high risk or equity mortgage, is rarely used for residential financing. Private and junior lenders issue them and they are sometimes referred to as lenders of last resort. They provide mortgages when major lenders refuse or turn down the borrower's application. The high risk lender isn't restricted by the loan to value rules, as with the 75%, 90%, and the 95% values established by the previous two types of mortgages.

The premium interest rates and other charges, in the form of bonuses and arrangement fees, represent a major obstacle against their usage. When those charges are added as a borrowing cost, the effective rate of interest sometimes exceeds double or triple that charged for a conventional or insured mortgage. Published mortgage rates found in most daily newspapers don't apply to the high risk lender. Those lenders are found by contacting lawyers, mortgage brokers, and personal loan companies.

b. THE DIFFERENCE BETWEEN AMORTIZATION AND TERM

If you went to a loan company to borrow $5 000 to purchase a vehicle and the lender set up a monthly re-payment plan for three years, it means that at the end of the three-year period, you would own that vehicle free and clear of the debt. The term of the loan is three years because that is when the loan agreement expires. The amortization is three years as well, because that is the period of time it takes to pay the loan in full. In this case, both term and amortization coincide. Amortization doesn't mean term.

Since the mortgage term is the period of time the mortgage lender allows you to borrow money, regardless of how long it takes to pay the loan in full, then amortization is the length of time it is going to take to pay the loan off in full. When borrowing for a home, the loan value is generally much larger than when purchasing a vehicle. So at the end of the mortgage term there is usually a balance remaining that either must be paid in full, or the lender agrees to a further term by a renewal agreement.

If you were to set up a $100 000 loan at 10% and amortize it over the same three-year period, the monthly payments would be $3 217.24. The average purchaser couldn't possibly afford to pay that much every month. However, if you paid $894.49 each month, then you're arranging a $100 000 mortgage loan over a 25-year amortization period. In this case the amortization or length of time to pay the loan off is 25 years. Today, mortgage lenders rarely offer longer than 25-year terms. These are offered only in rare cases, where excess capital funds are available by investors wanting fixed rates for long periods.

41

Mortgage lenders as a rule commit their funds for short terms ranging from six months up to five years. They recognize that if the loan was paid over the same five-year term, only a handful of people could afford the mortgage. For instance a $100 000 mortgage loan at 10% repaid over five years means a monthly payment of $2 114.77. This amortization period is, therefore, too prohibitive. To make it possible for average home owners to afford the monthly payments, lenders offer the same $100 000 mortgage loan based on amortization periods of up to 25 years. The result is to lower the monthly payments to a manageable amount. In the example of the $100,000 loan at 10%, the monthly payment of $894.49 represents the minimum monthly payment, because it is based on a 25-year plan for paying the mortgage off. The term you may select is no more than five years. At the end of the term, the lender either calls in the loan or grants a renewal for a further term of up to five years. At each renewal date interest rates are based on the current rate prevailing at the time of renewal.

The maximum amortization period offered by major lenders is 25 years, which represents the lowest monthly payment purchasers can negotiate with lenders. As a result, amortization determines at any period in time the number of months it takes to pay the mortgage off, assuming a specified interest rate and monthly payment. The term, however, rarely coincides with the amortization, as with short-term vehicle loans. Under a mortgage, you're renegotiating your mortgage term and interest rate several times before the mortgage loan ever gets paid in full.

c. PRIVILEGES AND OPTIONS

1. Mortgage privileges

Mortgage privileges are rights extended to borrowers that are exercisable at the borrower's discretion. For example most conventional and insured mortgages contain a privilege allowing borrowers to pre-pay an amount once a year without having to pay a penalty. The amount is based on a percentage of the principal balance outstanding, equalling as much as 10% to 15%. It is non-cumulative, so that if you don't exercise the privilege in one year the pre-payment amount is lost and cannot be carried forward for purposes of adding it to the privilege for the following year.

Another very important privilege is where borrowers may pay off the mortgage loan at any time during the term without a penalty. Mortgages with this privilege are known as open mortgages. This is a privilege rarely granted by major lenders unless it is negotiated in advance, and the mortgage term as a rule is never longer than two years. Interest rates are higher for this privilege as opposed to closed mortgages.

An important privilege to keep in mind relates to insured mortgages. It is the right of the borrower to pay off the mortgage loan any time after three years into the term; this privilege is exercisable automatically on payment of three months' interest penalty. That is the maximum penalty lenders are permitted to charge without being in violation of CMHC policy. When the lender demands a larger pay out penalty — and incidentally this is happening frequently — object strongly or report the incident to the area office of CMHC for a correction.

2. Mortgage options

There are basically two mortgage options to understand. The most common option is the right to take your mortgage to another property you intend to buy after you have sold. This is referred to as the portable option. When the mortgage is transferred, the mortgage interest rate, monthly payment, principal amount, and the due date remain the same. It doesn't matter if interest rates currently charged are higher or lower than the mortgage rate.

In all cases where portable options are exercised, the purchaser has no alternative but to arrange his or her own mortgage financing to buy your property. See section **e.** in chapter 4: the first financing clause applies where purchasers arrange their own financing. Instruction is provided to show you how to complete the blank spaces for that clause.

Sometimes the financing amount you are transferring to the other property doesn't coincide with your financing needs. The mortgage amount you're transferring may either be not enough or more than you need to finance the new deal. In either case, you can make adjustments to the principal balance to suit your financing needs for the new purchase if the underwriting requirements of the lender are met, such as the loan-to-value rules that apply to different types of mortgages.

The second option is where the purchaser takes over your existing mortgage. This option is available under all types of mortgages unless a condition in the mortgage contract states that the purchaser cannot assume your mortgage. If nothing is set out that prevents purchasers from taking over your mortgage, then this option could automatically be exercised. By law, the lender has the right to still look to you for payment of the debt if the purchaser defaults under the mortgage contract.

Most mortgages contain a condition preventing purchasers from assuming mortgages unless they are approved by the lender. The approval process is similar to where the purchaser obtains a new mortgage loan. When approval is granted to assume, normally lenders will provide a written letter releasing you from further liability.

Five situations arise when purchasers assume your mortgage. In chapter 4, section **e.**, each situation is listed with its corresponding financing clause set out in the typical agreement of purchase and sale. Instructions on how to complete the blank spaces for each of the five clauses are provided.

d. NEGOTIATING TERMS AND RENEWALS IN ANTICIPATION OF SELLING

When arranging a mortgage on your property, you always select mortgage terms ranging anywhere from six months to five years. If you expect to sell in the near future, it is better to negotiate open mortgages or terms that coincide with your selling time table. Don't place much emphasis on current interest rates, even if they are starting to rise, unless you intend to transfer the mortgage to a new property you are purchasing. When you lock yourself into a longer term to protect against rising interest rates, you limit your options for avoiding a penalty. Penalties are a cost of borrowing and when they're added to the effective rate of interest, they're substantially higher than current rates charged in the marketplace. The same rule applies when your mortgage term is coming up for renewal, but you intend to sell your home; select either an open privilege or a short term that coincides with the time you intend to sell.

e. DIFFERENT WAYS TO AVOID SEVERE PENALTIES

The most obvious way to avoid a mortgage penalty is to have an open mortgage. Unfortunately, not everyone can anticipate exactly when they intend to sell, so longer terms are often negotiated to fix reasonable interest rates, especially if interest rates are rising. In many cases, selling results from a spur of the moment decision or circumstances beyond our control; it could be loss of a job, financial difficulties, additions to the family, promotion, or some other circumstance.

Examine your mortgage to determine if the portable option is available to allow you to transfer your mortgage to another property you intend to buy after the sale of your present home. By taking the mortgage with you, you have no need to pay it off; thus, you have avoided the penalty.

When it is not practical to transfer your mortgage to another property, examine the possibilities for the purchaser to assume your mortgage. Three conditions should be considered before relying on this method for avoiding a penalty. Ask yourself the following:

(a) Is the interest rate on my mortgage higher than the current rates charged in the market?

(b) Is there a condition in the mortgage contract preventing purchasers from assuming my mortgage apart from obtaining the lender's approval?

(c) By permitting the purchaser to assume, is there a good possibility for me to become liable to the mortgage lender if the purchaser defaults under this mortgage?

If the answer to the first two questions is negative, then this financing arrangement could provide a practical method for avoiding a penalty. When considering the last question, you only need to be concerned when you can't secure the lender's written release of liability. Examine the credit-worthiness of the purchaser and the value of your property over and above the mortgaging to determine your potential liability. Obviously, if the mortgage financing amount represents over 75% of your property's value, then potential for incurring future liability is more probable. Weigh each circumstance on its own merits before deciding on using this method to avoid a penalty. Consult your lawyer for help.

As a last resort for minimizing a severe penalty, you might consider utilizing the annual partial prepayment privilege if the timing of your sale is appropriate. Determine when the annual prepayment privilege is exercisable. Arrange for the sale of your home to coincide with the exercisable date, or if that isn't convenient, arrange to take out a short-term loan equal to the maximum amount of the prepayment privilege and exercise the privilege before the sale date. Pay the annual prepayment amount and later, when you pay the mortgage in full, the penalty will be calculated on a reduced balance, thus lowering the penalty amount otherwise payable.

In the next chapter, the financing clauses are provided. If you understand the preceding financing considerations, it will be easier to choose the appropriate clause in the real estate contract for your particular circumstances.

4

PUTTING IT IN WRITING

The agreement of purchase and sale is a document you must use for all residential property sales. This form is fairly standard throughout North America, although it varies in style and title depending on where you live. For instance, in British Columbia it is called the *contract of purchase and sale* or *interim agreement*, and in Ontario it is known as the *agreement of purchase and sale*. Pre-printed forms are available from the publisher (see the order form on page vii). They may also be available in stationery stores.

During the negotiations with potential purchasers, all the relevant terms and conditions are recorded in this agreement. Eventually, when all the conditions are removed, you arrange to deliver the agreement to the lawyers representing yourself and the purchaser, and they take the responsibility for finalizing the sale proceedings.

Review the following material several times to gain a working knowledge about completing the agreement of purchase and sale form. By familiarizing yourself now with the form from beginning to end, you'll empower yourself with confidence to conclude an agreement. Later, when you are face-to-face with the potential purchaser negotiating terms of the sale agreement, this document can then be completed and you won't lose momentum for selling.

A standard agreement of purchase and sale is shown in Sample #6. This agreement is for all residential properties except condominium and co-operative sales. To sell those properties, you need different forms; if necessary, consult your lawyer for copies.

Explanation for each section of the agreement is given below. Read carefully and make sure you understand what is required before you complete the form. In most cases, you'll probably find it unnecessary to consult a lawyer. However, whenever you're not quite sure about your position, seek legal advice. There is probably more comfort retaining a lawyer for the process of preparing the agreement, and in difficult circumstances it is probably a good idea. Generally, however, agreements are easy to complete when you know how; the saved time and extra legal costs justify completing the agreement yourself, especially when purchasers cool off quickly, and some are suspicious of one-sided legal representation. To get the most effective results, try preparing the agreement yourself and consult a lawyer only for back-up assistance when necessary.

a. IDENTIFYING THE PARTIES TO THE DOCUMENT (section 1)

The first section identifies the purchaser. Use full legal names and avoid nicknames or initials. The second section identifies the vendor. Vendors are correctly described by recording their full legal names exactly as they appear on the ownership document.

Other parties acquire rights to your property by virtue of their relationship with you, even though the ownership papers may have been registered in your name alone. So, for example, if the person you live with or your spouse acquire rights against your property, you'll need his or her consent in writing before you can sell it. Your spouse becomes a party and his or her name and signature must appear on the agreement form, even though your spouse's name may not be shown on the ownership document.

SAMPLE #6
AGREEMENT OF PURCHASE AND SALE

1. The undersigned _____

_____

(Insert purchaser(s) full legal name.)

having inspected the lands and premises described in this document and attached schedules if any, irrevocably offers to purchase from _____

_____

_____

(Enter the vendor's (seller's) name as shown on the ownership document and add any persons who have acquired an interest in your property.)

2. the lands and premises described

_____

_____

_____

(Enter the full legal description: if space insufficient, add a schedule.)

3. with the following restrictions_____

_____

_____

_____

(Enter all restrictions attached to the lands.)

Otherwise the property shall be accepted free from restrictions, charges, liens, claims,

Except for minor easements or agreements in favor of the municipality or any public or private utility including Bell Canada, provincial or local hydro, fuel, telephone, television, cable, sewers, water, municipal or other services for the supply of utilities to this property and adjacent properties.

And except restrictions and covenants that run with the land provided they are complied with.

4. The purchaser is not to call for the production of any title documents, or abstract of title, proof or evidence of title except such as are in the vendor's control.

5. The purchase price agreed to is_____

_____

_____Canadian dollars ($_____) .

6. The purchaser submits with this offer _____

Canadian dollars ($_____) payable to the vendor's lawyer in trust as a deposit pending completion or other termination of this agreement and to be credited towards the purchase price on completion.
(If deposit amount is to be increased after signing, then add the following clause:)

The purchaser agrees to submit a further sum _____

of _____ Canadian dollars ($_____) on or before _____19____ payable to the vendor's lawyer in trust as a further deposit pending completion or other termination of this agreement and to be credited towards the purchase price on completion.

7. The purchaser's lawyer shall have seven days from the date of acceptance to review this agreement, and in the event the purchaser's lawyer is unsatisfied with any terms of this agreement, a notice of objection may be served on the vendor within the seven days to null and void the agreement. Otherwise this condition is automatically waived.

8. The financing terms agreed to are as follows*:

(i) Where the Purchaser is arranging new financing;

This offer is conditional upon the purchaser arranging a new first mortgage for not less than _____ ($_____), The type of mortgage is a _____ mortgage, bearing interest at the rate of not more than _____% per annum calculated semi-annually not in advance and repayable in blended monthly payments of _____($_____), and to run for a term of five years from the date of completion of this agreement. This offer is conditional upon the purchaser obtaining the said mortgage by no later than _____ p.m. on _____ 19_____ otherwise this offer shall be null and void and the deposit(s) shall be returned in full without interest. This condition is inserted for the benefit of the purchaser and may be waived at the purchaser's option by notice in writing to the vendor within the time period.

* Select only one financing provision and cross out the remaining provisions with all parties initialing the changes.

(ii) (a) Where there is a straight assumption;

The purchaser agrees to assume an existing first mortgage
for approximately _____($_____),
bearing interest at the rate of _____% per annum
calculated semi-annually not in advance and repayable in
monthly payments of_____ ($_____),
including both principal and interest and due on the_____ day
of _____ 19____. This offer is conditional upon the
purchaser obtaining approval to assume the said mortgage by
no later than _____ p.m. on _____ 19_____
otherwise this offer shall be null and void and the deposit(s)
returned in full without interest.

*(ii) (b) Where the existing mortgage is assumed on the condition the
principal amount is increased;*

The purchaser agrees to assume an existing first mortgage
for approximately_____ ($_____),
bearing interest at the rate of _____% per annum
calculated semi-annually not in advance and due on the_____ day
of _____ 19____, provided that the mortgage principal amount
shall be increased by approximately_____
($_____) bearing interest at the rate of _____% per annum
calculated semi-annually and not in advance. The two financing
amounts to be combined into one mortgage amount. This offer
is conditional upon the purchaser obtaining approval to arrange
the said financing no later than _____ p.m. on
_____ 19_____ otherwise this offer shall be null and
void and the deposit(s) returned in full without interest.

*(ii) (c) Where the existing mortgage is assumed and the principal
mortgage amount is decreased;*

The offer is conditional on purchaser being approved to
assume an existing first mortgage for approximately
_____ ($_____), bearing
interest at the rate of _____% per annum calculated
semi-annually and not in advance, and repayable in monthly
payments of _____ ($_____), including
principal and interest and due _____ 19_____. This offer

is conditional upon the purchaser obtaining approval to assume the said mortgage by no later than _____ p.m. on _____ 19_____ otherwise this offer shall be null and void and the deposit(s) returned in full without interest.

(ii) (d) Where the existing mortgage is assumed and additional funds raised by a second mortgage with a third party lender.

The offer is conditional upon the purchaser being approved to assume an existing first mortgage for approximately _____ _____ ($_____), bearing interest at the rate of _____% per annum calculated semi-annually and not in advance, and repayable in monthly payments of _____ ($_____), including principal and interest and due _____ 19_____. This offer is further conditional upon the purchaser arranging a second mortgage for _____ ($_____) bearing interest at the rate of _____% per annum calculated semi-annually not in advance and repayable in blended monthly payments of _____ ($_____), including both principal and interest and expiring on the same date as the first mortgage. This offer is conditional upon the purchaser obtaining approval for the two financing arrangements by no later than _____ p.m. on _____ 19____. The financing condition is inserted for the benefit of the purchaser and may be waived at the purchaser's option by notice in writing to the vendor within the time period.

(ii) (e) Where the existing mortgage is assumed and additional funds are raised by the vendor taking back the second mortgage.

The offer is conditional upon the purchaser being approved to assume an existing first mortgage for approximately_____ _____ ($_____), bearing interest at the rate of _____% per annum calculated semi-annually and not in advance, and repayable in monthly payments of _____ ($_____), including principal and interest and due _____ 19_____. This offer is further conditional upon the vendor agreeing to

take back a second mortgage for _____ ($_____)
bearing interest at the rate of _____%per annum calculated
semi-annually not in advance and repayable in blended
monthly payments of _____ ($_____),
including both principal and interest and expiring on the
same date as the first mortgage. This offer is conditional upon
the purchaser obtaining approval to assume the said mortgage
by no later than _____ p.m. _____ 19____
otherwise this offer shall be null and void and the deposit(s)
returned in full without interest.

9. The purchaser and vendor agree that all existing fixtures are
included in the purchase price except for rented hot water heat-
ers and except those fixtures listed as follows:

_____

_____

_____

The following chattels shall form part of the purchase price and
the vendor warrants that the chattels are free from liens or en-
cumbrances:

_____

_____

_____

10. This agreement shall be completed on the _____ day of
_____ 19____ at which time vacant possession is to be given
to the purchaser unless part of the premises is rented to a third
party and the purchaser agrees to assume the tenancy. The covenants and conditions shall survive the completion date of this
agreement.

11. The purchaser is to be allowed twenty (20) days from the removal of all conditions to investigate the title at the purchaser's
expense, and if within such time the purchaser furnishes the vendor in writing with any valid objection to title or any outstanding municipal work order or municipal deficiency notice which
the vendor shall be unable or unwilling to remove and which

the purchaser shall not waive, this agreement shall be null and void and the deposit money(s) shall be returned without interest and the vendor shall not be liable for any costs or damages. Save as to any valid objection the purchaser shall be deemed conclusively to have accepted the title of the vendor to the property.

12. All buildings, fixtures, improvements and chattels being purchased shall be and remain at the risk of the vendor until completion of this agreement. The vendor shall hold all insurance policies and the proceeds payable from those policies related to the property being purchased which shall be held in trust for the parties as their interests may appear so that in the event of damage the purchaser may terminate this agreement and all deposit money(s) returned to the purchaser without interest or else take the insurance proceeds and complete the purchase.

13. The vendor warrants that the present use of the premises may lawfully be continued.

14. The vendor shall deliver on or before completion date a statutory declaration that the vendor is not a non-resident of Canada or alternatively, will supply the purchaser with the prescribed certificate that all liability for tax payable by the vendor under the non-residency provisions of the Income Tax Act by reason of this sale are satisfied. If the vendor fails to comply with this condition the purchaser shall be at liberty to hold back sufficient funds out of the proceeds of sale equal to thirty-three and one-third percent of the sale price and forward same to Revenue Canada or terminate this agreement with the return of the deposit money(s) without interest.

15. Any rents, mortgage interest, realty taxes including local improvement rates, hydro, water, gas, and fuel, shall be apportioned and allowed to the day of completion, the day of completion itself to be apportioned to the purchaser.

16. Any tender of documents or money may be made on the vendor or purchaser or their respective lawyers. Money may be tendered by bank draft or certified cheque by a Chartered Bank, Trust Company, Province of Ontario Savings Office, Credit Union or Caisse Populaire. All fees, levies or taxes in connection with the registration of the purchaser's documents shall be at the expense of the purchaser. The purchaser covenants to accept the transfer acceptable for registration, and any other documents related to this agreement, in accordance with the forms as prescribed by the vendor.

17. If the purchaser does not complete the purchase on the completion date or the extended completion date, as the case may be, the vendor may serve a written notice on the purchaser to perform the agreement. If the purchaser fails to complete the purchase after the receipt of the written notice, the deposit money(s) shall be forfeited to the vendor and the vendor may re-sell the property.

The re-sale of the property may be affected at a public auction, public tender or by private contract, and the deficiency, if any, occasioned thereby together with all loses, damages and expenses of the vendor shall be paid by the purchaser if a claim for such payment is made by the vendor, but any increase in the price obtained at the re-sale shall belong to the vendor.

18. Time in all respects shall be of the essence of this agreement.

19. The vendor represents and warrants that during the time the vendor has owned the property, the vendor has not caused any building on the property to be insulated with insulation containing urea formaldehyde, and to the best of the vendor's knowledge no building on the property contains insulation that contains urea formaldehyde. The warranty shall survive and not merge on the completion of this transaction, and if the building is part of a multiple building, the warranty shall only apply to that part of the building which is the subject of this agreement.

20. The purchaser is hereby notified and consents to the vendor obtaining a credit report containing credit and personal information in connection with this agreement.

21. Where a conflict exists between any provision written or typed in this agreement (including any schedules to this agreement) and any provision in the printed portion, the written or typed provision shall take precedence over the printed provision to the extent of such conflict. The agreement including any schedules attached shall constitute the entire agreement between the purchaser and the vendor. There is no representation, warranty, collateral agreement, or condition expressed or implied other than as expressed in this agreement. This agreement shall be read with all changes of gender and number required by the context.

22. Any notices required by this agreement shall be in writing and shall be given by delivering same or mailing same by prepaid registered mail to the purchaser and vendor at the address set out below and if delivered, be deemed to have been received by the purchaser or the vendor on the sixth day after the posting.

23. The purchase price stated herein is exclusive of any goods and services tax (GST) payable by the purchaser pursuant to the Excise Tax Act. The purchaser hereby agrees to pay to the vendor or otherwise as required by law, any such GST and, in the case where the purchaser is required by law to remit the GST directly to the Department of National Revenue, to provide the vendor with evidence of the purchaser's registration pursuant to the said Act and evidence of such payment.

24. This agreement shall be binding upon the parties and their respective heirs, executors, administrators and assigns.

DATED at _____, this ____ day of _____, 19____ .

SIGNED, SEALED AND DELIVERED
    in the presence of:

_____
   Witness

_____   _____
  Purchaser address   *Purchaser*

_____   _____
  Purchaser Address   *Purchaser*

_____   _____
  Lawyer Address   *Lawyer*

The vendor hereby accepts the above offer and promises and agrees to and with the purchaser to duly carry out the same on the terms and conditions above-mentioned.

DATED at _____, _____ this _____ day of _____, 19____.

_____
Witness

_____   _____
Vendor Address   *Vendor*

_____   _____
Vendor address   *Vendor*

_____   _____
Lawyer address   *Lawyer*

The parties hereby acknowledge having received a copy of this agreement dated the _____ day of _____ 19_____ .

If this applies to your situation, contact a lawyer for guidance. Don't risk a lawsuit by refusing or failing to recognize those who have acquired legal rights to your property. Identify them and make certain they're prepared to consent, in order to avoid a potential problem later.

b. PROPERTY DESCRIPTION AND RESTRICTIONS (sections 2 and 3)

Fill this section out immediately when you determine the legal description. The municipal address alone is insufficient because the size of the property and the property's location are not exactly ascertainable in every case. You avoid vagueness and confusion by using only the complete legal description; don't follow the practice of only including the approximate frontage and depth and an abbreviated version of the property's legal description.

The legal description gives the exact dimensions either directly or by reference. The property's location is determined from its legal description and there is no better way to accurately describe or determine its exact location, other than perhaps attaching a survey.

The ownership paper is your source for the legal description. Sometimes several pages are necessary to fully include it. When space is inadequate, write on the space provided in the form "as shown on schedule A attached hereto." This permits additional sheets to be attached to the agreement as long as they are properly labelled (e.g., page one of two of Schedule A) and signed by all parties. Those additional sheets then form part of the agreement. Complete this section now, so you don't have to worry about it later when you're negotiating strategy points with the purchaser.

Next, include all restrictions affecting title to the property. Restrictions should be entered on the agreement form immediately, so you don't have to dwell on this issue when you're actually negotiating the terms of the agreement.

Chapter 2 outlined how important it is to include restrictions in your agreement. They include anything affecting title that prevents purchasers from having all the rights customarily accepted with legal ownership. Leaving restrictions out of the agreement gives purchasers an option to abort the deal. For example, a right of way allowing others to pass through your property is a restriction which is almost impossible to get rid of. If purchasers are not informed in the agreement of purchase and sale of a previously established right of way, the chances of an aborted deal are almost certain. Subsequent negotiations are almost guaranteed to be at your expense to compensate the purchaser.

c. THE PURCHASE PRICE (section 5)

Purchase price is the total sum in dollars agreed upon between you and the purchaser. It is the total consideration calculated by adding the deposit, financing arranged and financing assumed, and the down payment. See chapter 11 for more about purchase price.

d. THE DEPOSIT (section 6)

The deposit is a sum of money given by the purchaser at the time of signing the agreement of purchase and sale showing his or her good faith. Those funds are held by or on behalf of you and are applied toward the purchase price when the deal is completed. The strategy of deposit negotiation is discussed in chapter 11.

e. FINANCING CONDITIONS (section 8)

The most frequently used financing clause is where the purchaser arranges new financing. The other less commonly used clause is where the purchaser takes over or assumes the existing mortgage on the property, usually because current interest rates for new financing are higher than the vendor's mortgage rate. Also, the vendor is spared a penalty by not having to pay the mortgage out. If the mortgage is being assumed, five possible situations arise depending on the circumstances (see section **2.** below).

In order to rely on the different financing clauses, the purchaser in most cases needs the mortgage lender's approval. Usually ten to 20 days, known as the conditional period, are given for this purpose. If the purchaser is unable to obtain the lender's approval, then the agreement falls through; the purchaser gets his or her deposit back without interest, and you must then put the house on the market again. However, if the financing is approved, the purchaser has to sign a waiver form removing the condition to finalize the sale. The waiver form is discussed in detail in chapter 12.

1. Where the purchaser is arranging new financing (section 8 (i))

This financing clause is based on combining the lowest interest rate and the lowest possible monthly payment offered by lenders, using the 25-year amortization as a base. The clause merely establishes minimums as a guide for the financing. Purchasers are still permitted to arrange their own terms and options with a lender, notwithstanding the conditions in this clause. For example, a mortgage could be negotiated for a higher monthly payment if the purchaser decided he or she wanted to pay off the mortgage sooner than the 25 years contemplated by the financing clause.

More importantly, the financing clause is used as a gauge for both you and the purchaser to determine the purchaser's ability to meet the financing clause for the conditional approval. It prevents the purchaser from setting up conditions that are impossible for lenders to meet, and thereby escape liability if they later decide they don't want the property.

To complete the first space in this financing clause, ascertain the total financing needed by the purchaser. This is calculated by subtracting the down payment and the deposit(s) from the purchase price. The down payment is the purchaser's net savings left to apply toward the purchase price after paying for the appraisal fee, legal fee, survey fee, taxes, and other associated costs. Provide your interested purchasers with a list of estimated costs (see chapter 6). Enter the purchaser's financing amount in the first space provided.

Next, make an examination to determine the type of mortgage the purchaser wants. Is it a conventional or insured mortgage? For new mortgage financing, purchasers don't normally go to high risk lenders unless all other avenues fail. After determining the type of mortgage (as explained in chapter 3), fill in the appropriate space with either "conventional" or "insured."

The interest rate, monthly payment, and due date of the mortgage needs to be determined to complete the following spaces. All three are connected by determining the best choice of combining the lowest interest rate and the lowest monthly mortgage payment as indicated earlier.

Generally, five-year mortgage terms offer the lowest interest rate by most lenders. For this reason, five years is chosen for the term in all new financing clauses. The interest rate is determined from five-year mortgage terms based on the type of mortgage selected. The source for quoting interest rates is your weekly interest rate journal if you've kept it up-to-date, or contact a conventional lender for the current five-year rate based on the type of mortgage. Enter the rate in the following space provided.

The lowest monthly payment depends on the amortization chosen — the length of time it takes to pay the mortgage off if monthly payments and interest rates remain constant over the total period. Another way of looking at it is that the longer it takes to pay the mortgage off, the lower the payment is. Since the longest amortization period offered by most lenders is 25 years, the lowest monthly payment can be calculated by referring to a 25-year amortization table as shown in Table #1. This table gives interest rates ranging from 6% to 20%.

Follow through the table until you locate the quoted interest rate. The figure shown in the column beside the rate is the monthly payment for every $1 000 of financing. Divide the total financing amount by 1 000 and multiply its result by the figure beside the interest rate. The calculation provides the lowest monthly mortgage payment for the total financing based on a 25-year amortization.

To illustrate exactly how it works, take for example a $100 000 sale. If the purchaser's savings are $19 500, with buying costs of $3 000, $16 500 is then left over to use as a down payment toward the purchase price. The remaining $83 500 is financing needed by the purchaser to complete the deal. The insured mortgage is the only type available in these circumstances. Select the five-year insured mortgage rate if it is currently at 8%, then look through Table #1 until the interest rate of 8% is found. Beside the figure 8% is the amount $7.64 representing the amount of monthly payment for every $1 000 of financing. Calculate the monthly mortgage payment by multiplying the monthly payment for every $1 000 (7.64) times the amount needed for financing per $1 000 (83.5):

$7.64 x 83.5 = $637.94

This is the lowest monthly mortgage payment offered by most lenders.

Get in touch with a conventional lender in your area to find out how long it takes for purchasers to receive approval for financing; then enter the time you're prepared to give for obtaining the mortgage approval. The other financing clauses do not apply when new financing is arranged and should be crossed out.

2. **Where the purchaser takes over the vendor's existing financing (section 8 (ii))**

When your mortgage is being assumed, both parties must agree to this financing arrangement for it to work. Then you

TABLE #1
AMORTIZATION TABLE

INTEREST RATE %	COST PER 1 000 1 000
.06	6.40
.0625	6.55
.0650	6.70
.0675	6.86
.07	7.01
.0725	7.16
.0750	7.32
.0775	7.48
.08	7.64
.0825	7.80
.0850	7.96
.0875	8.12
.09	8.28
.0925	8.45
.0950	8.62
.0975	8.78
.10	8.95
.1025	9.12
.1050	9.29
.1075	9.46
.11	9.63
.1125	9.80
.1150	9.98
.1175	10.15
.12	10.32
.1225	10.50

TABLE #1 — Continued

INTEREST RATE	COST PER 1 000
%	1 000
.1250	10.68
.1275	10.85
.13	11.03
.1325	11.21
.1350	11.39
.1375	11.56
.14	11.74
.1425	11.87
.1450	12.10
.1475	12.29
.15	12.47
.1525	12.65
.1550	12.83
.1575	13.01
.16	13.20
.1650	13.56
.17	13.93
.1750	14.30
.18	14.67
.1850	15.04
.19	15.41
.1950	15.78
.20	16.15

Note: *the above table is based on a 25-year amortization.*

determine which of the five following financing clauses applies to your circumstances.

(a) Where there is a straight assumption (section 8 (ii)(a))

The straight assumption is where purchasers agree to assume your financing exactly according to its terms and the mortgage amount outstanding. Refer to your mortgage verification form (see Sample #4) for the information needed to complete the spaces for this clause. Enter the mortgage amount, interest rate, monthly payment, and the due date in the appropriate spaces provided.

The purchaser needs time to get the lender's approval — ten to 20 days is normally sufficient for this period. Enter in the space the time you are prepared to give for this purpose.

If you use this type of financing arrangement, you need a written release from the lender to avoid the potential for a future liability, even though you've sold the property and the purchaser received approval from the lender to assume your mortgage. Mortgage lenders don't give releases automatically — you will need to request it.

(b) Where the existing mortgage is assumed on the condition the principal amount is increased (section (8)(ii)(b))

This clause is used where purchasers assume your financing, but the mortgage principal amount is not enough and your lender agrees to increase the mortgage amount in order for the purchaser to have enough funds to complete the deal.

Since the mortgage is being assumed, refer to the mortgage verification form (see Sample #4) by entering the mortgage amount, interest rate, monthly payment, and due date. Next, calculate the additional financing needed by the purchaser. By adding the purchaser's down payment and deposit, plus the mortgage amount being assumed, and by subtracting the total from the purchase price, you determine the additional financing needed by the purchaser to complete the deal. As soon as this is determined, enter it in the space provided.

Refer to your weekly interest rate journal for the current rate of the type of mortgage being assumed. Select the current rate of interest based on the number of years remaining on the mortgage, and fill in the rate. Finally, fill in the time you are prepared to give the purchaser to obtain mortgage approval to complete this financing arrangement.

There is no need to obtain a release of liability from the lender with this type of arrangement because in order to increase the principal mortgage amount, a new mortgage has to be created displacing the original mortgage contract. Since you signed only the original mortgage contract, there is no possibility for the lender to look to you for payment in the future if the purchaser defaults.

(c) Where the existing mortgage is assumed and the principal mortgage amount is decreased (section (8)(ii)(c))

This clause is used when purchasers agree to assume your mortgage but they don't need the total financing amount, presumably because they want to put more money into the down payment. For this arrangement, you will likely have to pay a penalty because the mortgage principal amount has to be reduced to accommodate the purchaser. The penalty in this case is negotiable depending on the amount of reduction and the current interest rates prevailing in the marketplace. Contact your lender first to determine the penalty before you agree to the arrangement.

Fill in the details of the mortgage from your mortgage verification form (see Sample #4) to complete the blank spaces for the interest rate, monthly payment, and due date. Since the mortgage amount is reduced, only enter the amount required by the purchasers in the space provided. To finish this financing arrangement, enter the time you're prepared to give the purchaser for obtaining mortgage approval.

You need a written release of liability from the mortgage lender to avoid the potential for future liability on the mortgage contract.

(d) Where the existing mortgage is assumed and additional funds raised by a second mortgage with a third party lender (section (8)(ii)(d))

This financing clause applies when the purchaser assumes your financing but additional funds increasing the principal mortgage amount are not available from your lender. The purchaser then relies on a third type of mortgage (issued by high risk or junior lenders) known as equity mortgages.

This financing clause is split into two parts. The first is the assumption of your mortgage; this is exactly the same as in the straight assumption clause. Refer to your mortgage verification form (see Sample #4) to get the details for filling in the blanks for this part. To complete the second part for arranging the second mortgage, you need to determine the mortgage amount, interest rate, monthly payment, and the term. This is similar to arranging new financing as discussed in the first financing clause.

To calculate the financing amount needed for this part, add the purchaser's deposit and down payment together with the amount of mortgage being assumed and subtract the total amount from the purchase price. The remainder is the additional funds needed by the purchaser. Enter this amount in the space provided; then all you need to do is determine the interest rate, monthly payment, and the term.

Contact a mortgage broker or a lawyer whose specialty is arranging secondary financing and explain the purchaser's circumstances to obtain an interest rate quote for the situation. If the purchaser agrees with the quoted rate enter it in the space provided.

Once the rate is determined, it is easy to calculate a monthly mortgage payment. Refer to Table #1. Find the quoted rate. Immediately beside the rate is the amount of payment for every $1 000 of financing. Divide the financing amount by 1 000; multiply by the figure appearing beside the quoted rate to obtain the minimum monthly mortgage payment. Enter the monthly payment figure in the space provided.

Use the same due date as used for the mortgage that is being assumed. That way both mortgages expire at the same time. After entering this date, follow the same procedure as in the preceding clause by giving the purchaser time to get mortgage approvals. Enter the time you are prepared to give in the last space to finish the financing clause.

As with the straight assumption clause, you need to obtain from your lender a written release of liability in order to avoid any potential liability under the mortgage contract in a sale situation.

(e) Where the existing mortgage is assumed and additional funds are raised by the vendor taking back a second mortgage (section (8)(ii)(e))

In this situation, the purchaser assumes your existing mortgage financing and you agree to provide additional financing by taking back a second mortgage, normally as a last resort, in order to put a deal together. Again the financing clause is broken into two parts as in the preceding clause.

The information for the first part is exactly as in the preceding clause where you obtain the details from the mortgage verification form (see Sample #4) and enter the particulars of the mortgage amount, interest rate, and monthly payment in the spaces provided. For this financing arrangement you also need to give purchasers time to obtain mortgage approval.

Not having the lender's written release of liability doesn't matter under this arrangement, because by providing part of the financing on a second mortgage take back, you are assuming some risk in any case. If default occurs in the payments, you have the option of selling the home again under your rights contained in the second mortgage.

To complete that part of the clause relating to the second mortgage back to you, calculate the amount of financing needed by the purchaser by adding the purchaser's deposit and the down payment, plus the first mortgage amount assumed, and subtract the total amount from the purchase price. The remainder represents the additional financing you are providing the purchaser by a second mortgage to complete the deal. Enter the amount in the first space provided.

The information for completing the remaining spaces is similar to the second part of the preceding financing clause. Negotiate the interest between you and the purchaser, and enter it in the appropriate space provided.

The monthly payment is calculated by locating the agreed interest rate in the table of rates shown in Table #1. Follow through the table until you find the interest rate. The figure in the second column opposite it is the monthly payment for every $1 000 of financing. Divide the second mortgage financing amount by 1 000 and multiply the result by the interest rate in the table. This is the monthly mortgage payment for the second mortgage. Enter the monthly payment in the space provided.

Once the mortgage amount, interest rate, and monthly payment are entered, use the same expiry or due date for the mortgage being assumed. Both mortgages will then expire simultaneously. All that remains is to give the purchaser time for obtaining the mortgage lender's approval. Enter the time you're prepared to give to complete the financing clause.

f.   FIXTURES AND CHATTELS (section 9)

Fixtures are considered those items forming part of the realty, while chattels are items of a personal nature other than part of the real property.

If something is a fixture, it must stay as part of the real estate deal for the benefit of the purchaser. If it is a chattel, the vendor takes it with the rest of the furniture. When it comes to furnaces, doors, windows, kitchen cupboards, light fixtures, locks, and keys, it is easy to conclude they are fixtures because clearly they're intended to remain with the property for the benefit of the purchaser.

But what about curtain rods, mirrors, pool equipment, window screens, etc? The distinction isn't quite as obvious without applying proper rules. There are rules depending on the circumstances of each case. A helpful rule, in many cases, is to determine if the item is intended for temporary convenience — then it is a chattel. But if the item is intended to be used for enhancing the property's value, then it is a fixture.

Since there is no uniformity in the rules, you are advised to always identify questionable items in the agreement as an exclusion, if you intend to remove them from the deal. Therefore, the only way to keep a fixture such as a chandelier is to specifically write in the space provided that it is excluded from the deal.

Chattels included in the deal should be listed in the space provided. Confusion is avoided if you accurately describe each chattel by identifying its color, model, and make. When this is not possible, describe its location and some distinguishing mark.

g. THE CLOSING DATE (section 10)

The closing date is the date you intend to give up possession and keys to your property. It is set by agreement between you and the purchaser. The closing formality actually takes place at the office of public records where the lawyers make the exchange of documents, money, and keys. You may or may not be invited to the meeting for the exchange, but it is not necessary to be present; you can be busying yourself attending to more pressing matters and leave the closing formalities to your lawyer. For further discussion on the closing date, see chapter 11.

h. THE PARTIES' SIGNATURES

The final part of the agreement provides for the signatures. The first space is to enter the place where the agreement is made along with the day, month, and year. Next, the purchasers sign the form. If there is more than one purchaser and if only one is signing at a time, have each purchaser place beside their signature the date they signed the document.

Although it is not necessary to have the signature of a witness to legally bind the purchaser, it is still advisable. A third party, such as a relative or neighbor over 18 years of age, present as a witness provides proof that the person shown as the purchaser actually did sign the document on that date. Below the acceptance part, you and other parties having an interest in your property must sign the document to formally accept it.

The same witness may be used for all signatures as proof of signatures and formal acceptance. If additional sheets are attached to the document, they must be signed by all of the parties, including the witness(es).

The agreement is then formally personalized as your agreement of purchase and sale subject to the conditions noted in it. The rights and obligations contained in this document will eventually be reviewed by the purchaser's lawyer, the lender, and your lawyer. After you have negotiated any changes, and all parties agree, the agreement can be completed and signed (see chapter 11).

5

GETTING LEGAL HELP

It is almost impossible to successfully sell your home without getting some legal help. Keep in mind the important attributes of knowledge, experience, and availability. When you seek legal advice, determine what the lawyer's role in the selling process should be before you needlessly spend your hard earned money.

a. HOW TO CHOOSE A LAWYER

Most property owners have had experience dealing with lawyers; it would be difficult to own a home without having some minimal contact with the legal profession. When you decide to sell privately, a reliable real estate lawyer is probably one of the few people whose advice you can rely on. Your involvement with lawyers may be more intense because you are selling your home yourself, but by following the procedures in this book, you will be able to use that contact to your benefit. Questions will come up, so choose a lawyer who is available on short notice, especially for questions arising from the negotiation of an agreement of purchase and sale or an interim agreement.

You may have questions about a financing arrangement or some aspect of the standard agreement of purchase and sale form. To obtain a working knowledge of the selling process, you need to ask questions. It is not necessary to understand the legal ramifications arising out of every circumstance, but if you are in doubt, ask a lawyer with specialized training in real estate, not some other branch of the law. No single lawyer can be thoroughly knowledgeable about all areas of law, that is why specialization is stressed. Nevertheless, some lawyers haven't taken it upon themselves to restrict their services to specific areas. Therefore, I caution you to enquire about their experience and expertise in real estate matters.

When choosing a lawyer, ask for a list of all your anticipated costs before retaining their services. At the same time obtain a list of the potential costs the purchaser is likely to incur to buy your property. You may need to give the lawyer an approximate selling price so he or she can provide this list. Of course, this is only an estimate, but it will prove very helpful for purchasers who need that information to determine their down payment, as we discussed in previous chapters.

As tempting as it may seem, don't run to a lawyer every time questions come to mind. It could prove expensive, not to mention the annoying effect of repeated interruptions on the lawyer and his or her staff. When questions present themselves, get into the habit of writing them down, so that you can deal with all your questions at one meeting.

b. QUESTIONS ON DISCLOSURE

How much information should you disclose to purchasers in a sale proceeding? There is some information you may be reluctant to disclose, especially if the purchaser is not likely to find out before the deal closes. For example, what if your finished basement has a huge crack allowing moisture to seep in during heavy rains? Suppose there are contaminated substances buried on your property, slowly leaching to the surface and creating the potential for health problems? What if the well on your property runs dry during the warm season requiring great expense for trucking water? Until recently, buyers had little recourse from these problems, because they were expected to inform themselves by making appropriate inspections before signing any legal agreements. They had to overcome the umbrella rule that applies to all purchasers: buyer beware.

Recently, however, courts seem to be saying that vendors have responsibilities, too. They cannot be silent, nor can they actively conceal material defects from purchasers who, acting reasonably, couldn't be expected to discover them. Agents, as well as vendors, have been found liable when they entered into a scheme of concealment with each other.

In an effort to avoid these problems, agents in some areas ask vendors to answer a series of questions about the particulars of their property. The property disclosure statement contains one or more pages with a series of questions to be answered and signed by the vendor.

Purchasers are bound to come across property disclosure statements because they generally deal with real estate agents before they deal with you. You might be requested to supply one of these statements by an interested purchaser. Sample #7 shows a typical disclosure document. If you are comfortable with completing it, have one available in case it is requested by an interested purchaser. By producing this document on request, you're eliminating another objection purchasers put forth as a condition for making an offer. If you feel uncomfortable answering the questions listed in the property disclosure document, consult your lawyer for advice.

Alternatively, you could give a declaration to purchasers in the agreement of purchase and sale that you know of no relevant fact about your property that would significantly lower its value or significantly increase the ownership expenses. Such a declaration is used by the Quebec Real Estate Association for handling concealment issues. Including a declaration to purchasers in the agreement of purchase and sale probably more than satisfies most purchaser's concerns about material concealment.

c. THE LAWYER'S ROLE

Since you are selling you home privately, what role should lawyers play in the actual sale proceedings? They are certainly

SAMPLE #7
PROPERTY DISCLOSURE STATEMENT

Date of disclosure _____

The following statement is made by the vendor concerning the condition of the property located at:

_____

1.   Where there is only one owner: Have you lived on this property with your husband/wife at any time in the past?____

2.   Is there a plan of survey prepared by a surveyor showing all buildings and their locations relative to the lot lines?_____

3.   If yes, what is its date?_____

4.   If no, provide a rough sketch on the back of this sheet.

5.   What is the zoning?_____ Is the property zoned for its existing use? If yes, do building locations meet by-laws?____
If no, is it a legal non-conforming use?_____

6.   Other than minor easements to public utilities and Bell Canada, are there other easements affecting the property?_____
(For example: mutual driveway, rights of way, major hydro easements and storm sewer easements) If yes, describe the easements:

_____

7.   Are there building or other restrictions prohibiting, for example: TV antennas, above-ground pools, clotheslines, year-round use of recreational property, etc.? If yes, describe the restriction:

_____

8.   Is the property connected to a municipal water service? __
If no, describe the source of water:_____
Is the water plentiful?_____
Is the water potable?_____
Well depth?_____ Drilled?____ Dug?___

9.   Is the property connected to municipal sanitary sewers?___
If no, how is sewage disposed?_____ If septic tank and field bed: Are there any problems?_____ Provide a sketch showing the approximate location of the tank and field bed. When was the septic tank last pumped?_____

10.   Are you aware of any problems with the following:
a) electrical system?_____ b) heating system?_____

c) plumbing system?_____ d) roof?_____ e) basement moisture?_____ f) any other fixture or equipment?_____ If yes, describe_____

11. Age of furnace?_____ Age of roof?_____

12. Are you aware of any local improvement taxes?_____

13. Is the property or any part of the premises rented?_____ If yes, give particulars:_____ Can vacant possession be assured on the completion date?_____

14. ENVIRONMENTAL CONCERNS: Are you aware of any of the following: a) soil contamination?_____ b) asbestos?_____ c) radon?_____d) methane?_____e) underground petroleum tanks?_____ f) land fill substances under the ground?_____ g) is the property subject to flooding?_____

15. Are you aware of any problems with the swimming pool or hot tub?_____. If yes, give particulars_____

16. Are you aware of any structural problems? _____

17. Are all warranties affecting this property and the equipment transferable?_____

18. What is the approximate age of the home?_____

ADDITIONAL COMMENTS OR EXPLANATIONS_____
_____
_____

As a vendor, I warrant the above questions have been answered truthfully to the best of my knowledge. There are no other relevant facts pertaining to the property, its conditions or title which adversely affect the property. I agree that this disclosure may be shown to a prospective purchaser. In the event I become aware of additional information regarding this property at any time prior to the completion date I will notify the purchaser of same.

_____	_____	_____
Witness	*Vendor*	*Date*
	_____	_____
	Vendor	*Date*

not expected to be business advisers, price negotiators, or appraisers, those are areas for other trained professionals. Therefore, limit their services to questions of a legal nature. The following is a guideline as to when their expertise should be sought:

(a) Supplying specific wording for a clause you're having trouble composing

(b) Determining if other persons have acquired rights to your property

(c) Providing the legal description and restrictions for your property

(d) Assistance and advice regarding the legal implications when negotiating a particular mortgage financing clause in the agreement of purchase and sale

(e) Assistance and advice with fixtures and chattels forming part of the sale transaction

(f) Assistance and advice dealing with information you feel uncomfortable disclosing to purchasers

(g) Providing a list of yours and the purchaser's anticipated costs associated with the sale of your property

(h) Advice and assistance with any legal question you're concerned about

Of course, your lawyer's assistance goes beyond the above when he or she is given the agreement of purchase and sale after all conditions are satisfied or when the agreement is unconditional. Your lawyer is more actively involved because he or she takes charge of the transaction from there. Your lawyer takes care of the following:

- prepares the appropriate documents for transferring title

- conducts communications between other lawyers, municipal officials, and mortgage lenders to assemble information, and

- prepares an accounting to adjust such things as municipal taxes, etc.

Your lawyer is generally there to protect your interests, facilitate the transaction, and eventually attend to the formal closing by exchanging title documents and keys for money.

Now, after considering the legal help, it is time to enquire into the method for setting an asking price for the sale of your home.

6

HOW TO SET YOUR ASKING PRICE

Everybody wants as much as possible for their property. However, put a value on your home that will give you the best return and still ensure a sale. Difficult as it may seem, factors such as inflated ideas of value, sentimental attachment, and unease about making major decisions should not play a role in the price-setting process.

Setting the price for your home is a big psychological step. It is a time when you must turn off emotional switches and adopt a rational business approach. It is not what you think your property is worth that matters, it is what a willing purchaser is prepared to pay in a competitive marketplace that counts. After reading this chapter, you'll know how to set an offering price and not have to rely solely upon one real estate agent's advice.

Setting a price is not an exact science, although there are certain rules you must follow. If you act on a hunch, you may fall into a scenario like this: "Let's ask for as much as possible — if it is too high we can always drop our price." With this kind of thinking, the price is always set higher than the market range. If a lower price is offered, panic sets in because you lack the knowledge necessary to determine your price range and the ability to employ the negotiating strategies. Caution overrules, emotions run wild, and it is almost impossible to make a confident, rational business decision. In the meantime, the purchaser is off buying a similar property elsewhere. Time is beginning to run out before the stigma of "that high-priced property" causes the "for sale by owner" sign to come down, along with your high hopes.

Derailment in the selling process occurs because, rather than applying good business judgment, ignorance tempered with irrational emotion rules the day. Failed vendors with genuine motivation are the prime targets for the enthusiastic salesperson. All such vendors need is the calm reassurance of a fresh approach, and with little or no persuasion, the failed vendor agrees to set a lower price solely on the advice of the agent. If the agent is on the right track, the home eventually sells. Had the vendor known, all that commission money would have been his or hers instead of the agent's.

How does one acquire knowledge about the market? Your selling price should closely approximate what your property will bring in the market, allowing a slight margin for negotiating. Market value is generally viewed as the highest price a property will bring to a willing seller if exposed for sale on the open market, allowing reasonable time to find a willing purchaser. The emphasis here is placed on *willing purchaser*. What is the highest price you can set and still attract the willing purchasers? To find the answer, you must study the market firsthand and be willing to acknowledge the wisdom and expertise of those whose living depends on making the best estimates of value. When you combine firsthand knowledge with the assistance of experts, the odds favor you in determining the highest price a willing purchaser is going to pay.

Back in chapter 2, I suggested visiting similar homes for sale in your area. Drive around your neighborhood and jot down all the addresses and phone numbers shown on the "for sale" signs of homes similar to yours, if you haven't already done it. Contact each responsible person to obtain the following:

(a) selling price,

(b) dimensions of the lot,

(c) building size and type,

(d) general condition,

(e) special features, and

(f) the approximate length of time the property has been on the market.

Set the information in the journal where you are keeping track of current mortgage rates. Request a personal inspection of each home to fill in unanswered questions. After inspection, make your comparison objectively, comparing price and particulars against your property to determine which one is superior. Note your impressions beside each property. Those properties on the market for a long period are either over-priced or not properly marketed. Eventually, as you compare a number of similar properties, a pattern begins to emerge.

The next step is to contact three separate real estate offices in your area. Arrange for them to make an appointment to come to your residence for the purpose of providing an estimated selling price. Ask how much commission is charged under multiple listing. Most agents quote lower fees for an exclusive listing, but under a multiple listing service the percentage is higher because the property listing is circulated through all the participating real estate offices in the area under a commission sharing basis. The commission rate plus the tax is your savings if you decide to sell privately.

Good agents ask lots of questions. This provides an excellent opportunity to test your resolve. If a number of questions cannot be answered, you have more homework to complete. After the "questioning period," the representative goes to his or her office to conduct a computer search for comparable homes either recently sold, currently on the market, or both. When they return to your home, their estimates should be based upon a reconciliation of properties similar to yours. Consideration will be given to current trends in the marketplace; a recent shutdown by a major employer, or a sharp increase in mortgage lending rates affects trends and could influence any ultimate estimates of value. By asking questions, you can determine the factors that had the greatest influence on each agent's decision. Not all real estate agents are influenced by the same factors. That is why you rarely receive three identical estimates.

Agents should be able to tell you the average length of time it takes to sell your property under a multiple listing service. For their members, multiple listing services publish statistical information giving the average turnaround time. This time is short during economic booms and longer during recessionary periods.

The three estimated selling prices plus your research should provide a market range. However, remember that expert appraisers provide exclusively written independent estimates of market value for vendors, mortgage lenders, land assemblers, developers, and governments. Consult this professional whose name appears in the phone book under the category "appraiser." Those with an accredited real estate appraisal designation are not to be confused with real estate agents who hold themselves out to be residential appraisers. Contact at least two, determine their fee for providing a written appraisal report, and choose one. Make certain the appraiser knows that the function of the appraisal is for "sale purposes" only; appraisers' estimates of value differ depending upon the terms of engagement. If they're hired by mortgage lenders under power of sale proceedings because of a default under a mortgage, then the appraiser's opinion of value is more conservative than an appraisal for an unforced sale.

Appraisal reports are prepared in a professional standardized format that is easily understood. Consideration is given to many factors, not simply the comparison approach used by real estate salespeople acting as appraisers. Sometimes other approaches to value, such as actual cost to build or replacement cost may be more appropriate than a comparative value approach commonly relied on in less sophisticated estimates. The circumstances of each case dictate the most appropriate valuation method given the greatest weight for determining value. Social, economic, and physical factors are also taken into consideration before the final estimate is given by the professional appraiser.

These written appraisal reports contain detailed information identifying, in an objective way, all of the accepted approaches for determining market value to help you arrive at a rational valuation. In the report, the appraiser reveals the rationale for arriving at the opinion. The cost to obtain one of these detailed reports is surprisingly cheap: in most provinces they can be negotiated for under $300. A favorable appraisal report impresses potential purchasers because it gives them some assurance that the value is there, justifying the fact they're spending money wisely.

Now is the time to make your reconciliation of those estimates of value you've received from the real estate agents and the professional appraiser. Determine the spread from the four figures, the lowest to the highest. This gives you a marketability range, unless one of the figures is completely out of whack with the others; in that case, ignore it. Determine your price according to the closest grouping of figures, then allow a slight amount for negotiating.

Suppose, for example, you received the following estimates: $128 000, $130 500, $132 000, and $136 000. The closest grouping is $130 500 and $132 000 within the marketability range of $128 000 and $136 000. If you used $131 000 as the closest grouping and then added $2 500 for negotiating, you would accordingly set your sale price at $133 500, based on the information you received from the real estate agents and the professional appraiser.

If your investigation shows a number of comparable properties very similar to yours, consider setting your offering price within the marketability range, but slightly below the competition to give yourself a price advantage. This of course, depends upon whether the similar property is superior or inferior to yours. The object is to try to set your price so that other properties tend to sell yours, rather than vice versa. If there are no comparable properties, more weight should be given to the professional appraiser's estimate, because real estate agents rely heavily on comparable property values. Try finding a grouping around the professional appraiser's estimate for the marketability range and then set your price accordingly.

As previously stated, estimating an offering price is not a precise science, but by taking into consideration the opinions provided by the independents with experience and expertise, your marketability range is predictable with surprising accuracy. Now you're equipped to ascertain a proposed selling price without having to rely solely upon the judgment of one salesperson. During the whole selling process, continue monitoring the market by taking into consideration economic factors, such as a sudden shift in mortgage rates, and competition coming onto the market.

After talking with three real estate salespeople, you can judge for yourself if selling privately is for you. If you've decided it is not, at least you've learned how to set your selling price independently without relying completely on one person's estimate. Let's now consider how you are to make a commitment to a new accommodation.

7

MAKING A COMMITMENT TO
NEW ACCOMMODATION

What is the motivation behind selling your home? Surely selling, especially selling privately, fulfills a certain desire, and it is important to clarify your reasons for putting the house on the market now. Do you have the attitude and motivation to remain focused during the selling process?

If you're genuinely interested in selling, it is important for two reasons to make a conditional commitment to an alternative accommodation. The first reason is that your psychological motivation is reinforced once you take the further step of involving time and energy to find new accommodation. The second reason is that you're safely in a position to meet a time limit specified for giving possession to a purchaser who may need a home quickly.

If you make this conditional commitment for a new accommodation, and if it is arranged for an early closing, such as 60 days, then you can offer an early closing on your home, increasing the chances for a quicker sale. The "hot prospects" are always those who need a home in a specified time frame. The pressure of eroding time begins to weigh on them. By being in a position to accommodate them, you give yourself a positive edge for selling.

Most vendors know what they want after their home sells; they will either purchase again or choose a different life-style, like renting. When renting instead of buying, first consider your priority areas and rental cost. Canvas those areas by making enquiries from rental signs shown on properties. If your efforts yield little or no results, try rental agencies or real estate offices in the area.

When you've finally decided on the accommodation you are prepared to rent, try offering to lease once your home is sold. The deposit you submit with your application will be returnable if you haven't successfully sold within your time frame.

If you wish to purchase another home, the process is similar to finding rental accommodation. Visit areas you like, and jot down addresses and phone numbers of interesting homes for sale.

Contact two or three real estate offices to discuss your intentions and area of choice. When you find the property you're prepared to make an offer on, then make sure it is conditional on selling your home first. Make the offer conditional on financing as well.

Vendors want an escape clause in the agreement when you request conditions in the sale agreement; it gives them the right to continue offering the property for sale. In the event another satisfactory offer is received from someone else, you'll be required to decide (usually within 24 to 72 hours) whether to waive your condition or let the other person have the deal.

Never take the chance of possibly owning two homes at one time. In other words, don't waive conditions unless you're sure of having a binding agreement of sale for your home. Let me caution you again, never firm up an agreement to purchase another property when the sale of your home is not a "for sure deal." If the waivers for your home are signed removing conditions, or you are almost certain your deal is going to be finalized, then firm up the other deal. For example, suppose you have an accepted offer on your property subject to financing, and you've received verbal communications from the purchaser's lender stating the financing is approved, subject to written confirmation to follow in a few days.

By following the preceding steps, you have accomplished two things: you've made a commitment for an alternative accommodation subject to selling your home, and you have arranged your affairs to accommodate any purchaser's request for an early closing. The next chapter discusses the role real estate agents play in the selling of properties.

8

DEALING WITH REAL ESTATE AGENTS

Everyone involved in selling should have a general idea how real estate agents conduct their business. For the most part, members of this profession are salespeople paid on a commission basis. They must work hard, continually listing and selling properties to survive in a highly competitive business. Their industry has a number of associations, and each provincial real estate association sets minimum standards of professional conduct and ethics for its members.

For example, the hired salesperson keeps you informed and primarily protects your interests over the purchaser's, although they still have a duty to be honest and truthful about disclosing facts to the purchaser.

The words "agent" and "salesperson" are used as interchangeable terms by the public; most people in sales are referred to as agents. However, under agency law, the person who comes to your home for getting a listing signed is usually a salesperson, not the agent. Agents are brokers, the party you are contracting with under the listing agreement. Most likely, you'll have regular contact with the salesperson, or employee acting on behalf of the agent.

Do-it-yourselfers seeking to save money by selling their own home increase the competition real estate agents or salespeople face every day. Some agents may go to great lengths to convince you to deal with them rather than sell privately. So brace yourself for a variety of persuasive arguments and tactics meant to weaken your confidence by stressing your lack of knowledge and pointing out the potential pitfalls of lost time and money. Sometimes agents lead you to believe they have purchasers waiting to buy a property similar to yours. Some even go so far as to suggest that by selling your home privately you could be opening a window of opportunity to encourage criminal activities such as robbery and molestation. Salespeople with low ethical standards believe it is permissible to resort to this kind of conduct. Fortunately, most real estate agents have more integrity and will agree that it is your call to decide if you want to earn that commission.

Certainly, if you don't have the time or the selling acumen, then perhaps selling privately is not for you. There are excellent, hard-working real estate people willing to provide the kind of service you need.

If you decide to use an agent, you must sign a listing agreement. The gives the agent the authority to market your property and charge a commission. Unfortunately, it is difficult to find a list of the marketing services agents intend to utilize in selling your property. It is helpful to ask the following questions:

(a) How much advertising is anticipated over the listing period?

(b) Where is most of the advertising going to be concentrated?

(c) Are there specific groups he or she intends to target?

(d) How often will open houses be held for the public?

(e) How often will open houses be held for all agents in the area?

(f) Who is to have access to the property?

(g) When access is given, who is responsible for theft, loss, or damage?

(h) Will someone be providing feedback after a show-ing?

(i) How often will they be reviewing their marketing progress?

Request a written proposal covering your concerns, because even salespeople with good intentions sometimes forget what they promised after the listing agreement is signed. Remember, it is appropriate to expect to have guidelines setting out the marketing proposal they promised; it offers you accountability, and lets you know what to expect.

Good salespeople know the financial status of the average purchaser looking for a home in your neighborhood. After carefully examining your property and surrounding area, they can advise you of your selling features and any potential weaknesses that might prevent or impede a sale.

Enquire into the sales office's policy regarding the way exclusive listings are handled. In some offices they are jealously guarded so that other offices and their employees are not permitted to sell those properties; this situation may not be in your best interest.

Although commission percentages are generally higher for multiple listings as compared to exclusive agreements, there is at least the assurance of co-operation between all the participating offices affiliated with the listing board in your area. This type of listing offers a better chance for a quicker sale because more salespeople in the area have an opportunity to know and participate in the sale, which increases the chances for one of them to be working with a potential purchaser who might be interested in your property.

Good agents want to be with you during the presentation of all offers in order to protect your best interests. They often know the right questions to ask the other agent who is making the offer presentation, and that gives you the opportunity to make the best decision. Don't be afraid to ask questions and request your salesperson's opinion because effective agents are in for the long haul; they want your repeat business.

The sale of property through agents is a lucrative business. Salespeople realize that it is the vendor's interest they must protect, even though they often walk the fine line of trying to sell your property and at the same time assisting the purchaser to buy your home. Now is the time for you decide whether you are going to sell privately or hire an agent to conduct your sales program.

Although the remainder of this book is devoted to the do-it-yourself vendor, knowledge of the following material is helpful for anyone selling a home. Negotiating from a position of strength is necessary in all sales, regardless of your decision. The next chapter discusses the different ways to organize an effective advertising program.

9

ORGANIZING AN EFFECTIVE ADVERTISING PROGRAM

Advertising exposes your property to the market. There are no hard and fast rules — time, imagination, and innovation are what count.

The idea is to generate the greatest number of interested prospects in your price range within a budget of 8% to 10% of the estimated real estate commission savings. If, for example, the commission you would have paid to a real estate agent is $10 000, then budget a maximum of $1 000; that is more than enough to do the job. Set this amount aside for paid advertising, signs, and photocopying costs.

After talking to real estate agents, you probably determined the estimated time it takes to sell homes in your price range under multiple listings. For instance, if it takes four months to sell a home similar to yours plus an additional month for safety, you are allowing a total of five months to sell your property. After payment for the signs and photocopying, the balance should be divided by the number of weeks you estimate you will need to sell the property; this is your estimated weekly expenditure for paid advertising such as classified ads, magazine ads, radio spots, and television spots. Later, I'll discuss the costs and economic feasibility of using each type of paid advertising.

You may be surprised — the amount you budgeted for your advertising program is probably at least twice the amount real estate agents would spend to market your property. If your marketing expenditures are made wisely and effectively, you could keep part of those funds, especially if a sale takes place sooner than anticipated.

a. WORD OF MOUTH ADVERTISING

The moment you set your price, tell everyone that you're selling. "Word of mouth" is a powerful advertising tool. News of your selling travels fast and far. Who knows? Your potential purchaser might be a friend of a friend. Every day, make it a point to tell at least five new people. If they tell just two people who tell two more, then you can see it won't take long before a huge number of people know about your property. Don't miss out on this opportunity!

b. PREPARE AN ADVERTISING HAND OUT

An advertising "hand out" is a useful, inexpensive tool. Take a clear photograph of the front of your property no larger than 4 x 6 inches. An advertising hand out is shown in Sample #8. The actual document shouldn't exceed 8½" x 11", the size of a normal letter. Place the photograph at the top just below your address, purchase price, and financing terms (if applicable). Underneath, write a description of your property. It should be a brief paragraph of about 75 words and should include those features of your home that you believe will capture the imagination of a potential purchaser. Mention something special about your property, such as an attractive location. Keep the details brief — too much is as detrimental as too little. Give only enough information to arouse curiosity.

When you're satisfied with the contents of the advertising hand out, arrange to use a good quality photocopier to reproduce several copies. A clear photograph will reproduce adequately for your purposes.

Make copies available for friends, neighbors, co-workers, and the prospects who inspect your home through showings, either by open house or personal appointment.

15 WOOD AVENUE: $129 000

PHOTOGRAPH

(6" x 4")

Modern, one storey yellow brick ranch on quiet street near all amenities. This home is located approximately ten minutes from downtown; walking distance to the park, schools, library, and the university. The major shopping center is located within five minutes drive.

A high efficiency gas furnace was installed last year. The home is in excellent shape with a finished recreation room. The lot is large with a park-like setting.

7 rooms, one four-piece bath

and one three-piece bath

Lot size 60 x 130 ft.

Showings by appointment only. All offers in writing will be considered. For further information, **phone: 444-1226.**

c. PURCHASE A "PRIVATE FOR SALE" SIGN

Go to the local sign shop and purchase a "for sale" sign. It should be at least 24" x 22" and have the words "PRIVATE FOR SALE," with additional space for your phone number. The phone number should be large, clear, and visible from the street.

Place the sign on your front lawn so that it is visible from both directions. Avoid using hand-painted signs because they look unprofessional and amateurish. Sample #9 shows a suitable sign.

Remember, this sign is your cheapest and most effective advertising tool because it works for you 24 hours a day. Buy one that is durable and high quality.

d. HOLD AN OPEN HOUSE

You get to meet many different people at an open house. It is a tremendous vehicle for getting potential purchasers to see the property. The open house gives you the opportunity to advertise the interior layout and its appearance from the inside, as well as the rear yard features that are impossible to observe from the street. Open house is particularly important when the home's curb appeal is not so great; it becomes more important to have the home viewed throughout to be appreciated.

Make a commitment to hold open house at least one day for a few hours in the afternoon every weekend. Vendors serious about selling their home have shown that a rigidly maintained commitment to regular open house times invites more successful selling.

If you're proud of your home, then you're going to have a lot of fun showing it. Purchase as many open house signs as necessary to direct the main flow of traffic to your residence. They're relatively cheap since they only contain the words "open house" with an arrow. Position the open house

FOR SALE BY OWNER

PHONE 444-1226

Note: Minimum dimensions should be 24" x 22".

signs strategically at intersections to direct the flow of traffic to your home.

Open house is particularly advantageous in new subdivisions, because other homes in the area are being advertised constantly by builders and real estate agents alike. Don't miss an excellent opportunity like this; you have no advertising costs, because it is already being done by others in the area. Simply take advantage of your competitors' efforts, set up your open house signs, and wait for the prospects to come.

In growing communities, relocation is common; out-of-town buyers often spend weekends driving around to open houses. Place a small advertisement, showing the time and location of your open house in the local newspaper. It is worth it.

Open house is an invitation to the public to inspect your home, so keep your valuables out of sight and at all times have someone accompany the guests, as in a tour, through your home.

When you're busy with a number of guests, it is difficult to distinguish between the so called "tire-kickers" and the serious prospects. Don't be afraid to ask questions to determine what they're up to and why they're here. By screening and qualifying in subtle ways, you're not wasting time on those who have no intention to buy. It is fun trying to see if you can get your guests to disclose what they're up to. As your guests enter, make available your advertising "hand out" so they have something to read while they are waiting their turn. Also have a guest register handy for each person to enter their name, address, and phone number, so if someone becomes more interested as the tour progresses, you will be able to call them later and to ask what they think of your home and if they are interested in seeing it again at a private showing.

If questions from guests suggest they are interested, your potential purchasers may be a hot prospects. They may need to purchase a home within a relatively short period of time, ranging from immediately to as long as 180 days. Determine if their buying intentions are immediate or serious. Remember, don't let hot prospects slip away without getting a phone number; you'll want to call them later to arrange a private showing.

Don't miss the opportunity to take advantage of advertising by open house; it is cheap, a lot of fun, and it gets results.

e. TRY INNOVATIVE AND IMAGINATIVE ADVERTISING

If you've discovered you live in an area that is attractive to ethnic or religious groups, retired or working peoples, target that group by determining where they congregate. It could be a church, union hall, recreation center, factory, or some other place. Consider using your "hand out" as a flyer. Fold it twice and implement a blitz campaign by placing the flyers underneath the windshield wiper of all the vehicles parked in a lot where a target group is congregating.

If your research suggests your property might have speculative value desirable for a developer, builder, commercial or residential investor, then get a list of names and addresses from the phone book. Mail a short letter of enquiry to determine if they have any interest in your property. Advise them why you think your property has particular appeal for their purposes.

Sometimes nearby factories, shopping malls, laundromats, and other places supply bulletin boards so that people can advertise things for sale. Take advantage of this form of free advertising, especially if you are targeting first-time home buyers or retired couples.

f. SPEND WISELY ON PAID ADVERTISING

Apart from advertising your open house in the local newspaper, little of your budgeted funds have so far been spent on paid advertising — this is where your remaining weekly budgeted funds should be directed. There are many forms of paid advertising including classified ads in daily, weekly, bi-monthly, and monthly publications, as well as spots on radio and television. The question is where to spend the money most effectively; the answer is to follow the example of real estate agents, whose survival depends on making the best advertising choices. Through experience, they know the habits of the potential purchaser in your area.

Have you noticed that only a few agents advertise on radio and television, and very few advertise in monthly magazines? Obviously it is the return for the cost. Unless you have an expensive property, then it is probably not worth it. Television has recently gained more popularity in some areas of the country, but it is still very expensive, and one has to wonder if those spots are more beneficial to the agent's image than to the particular property that is being advertised.

Classified advertising is generally the cheapest and most effective medium for advertising on a limited budget. The publishers sell advertising space on a daily, weekly, and sometimes bi-monthly basis. Many real estate companies advertise in the classified section of appropriate newspapers and magazines. The most popular seem to be those weekly issues published primarily for "home sale" advertising. The issues are free and they're available at most convenience stores and shopping malls. Sometimes it is a matter of trial and error to determine the best publication to use in each area. However, if you study real estate agents in your area, you usually won't go wrong.

When composing an ad, keep it simple: you don't need a big expensive spread, smaller ones do just as well. Prepare at least three sample ads. Have a contest in your family for the one who composes the best three ads; for the winner, perhaps, a free night out to dinner or a movie. Alternate between one of the three ads so that the same ad doesn't appear for two consecutive weeks. See the three typical ads in Sample #10 for ideas. Try to be innovative and catchy, and by all means, be truthful and accurate. There are laws against misleading advertising. Every home has something special to offer; it could be a sun room, fireplace, oak trim, chandelier, bevelled glass, cathedral ceiling, large kitchen, close to the park, and so on. What attracted you to your home may also attract others. Arouse interest in your readers so that they make enquiries for more information.

Now you have some ideas to work on for setting up and organizing a good advertising program. Sometimes you may have to experiment, so don't tie yourself into a long-term advertising contract. Otherwise, you've lost flexibility, not to mention part of your budgeted funds if you sell faster than anticipated.

Advertising in itself doesn't sell properties, it merely provides you with an introduction to the potential purchaser. The rest is up to you to negotiate and put the deal together. Now let's go on to determine how to reap the benefits from your advertising program.

(a) **3 BEDROOM RANCH**
Move-in condition, recreation room,
new gas furnace, near park, $129 000
444-1226

(b) **15 WOOD AVE. $129 000**
3 bedroom brick ranch, large lot, fenced
yard, close to shopping   444-1226

(c) **PARK-LIKE SETTING**
Yellow brick, one storey, three bedroom
low heating costs, close to downtown,
$129 000   444-1226

10

REAP THE BENEFITS FROM YOUR ADVERTISING

The results of a good advertising program are manifested by the number and quality of enquiries you receive. Those enquiries originate mostly from phone calls, some by a knock at the door, and others by referral through friends. During the beginning phase of exposing the property to the market, there is generally a lot of interest and soon after the enquiries level off.

From the very beginning stage until you receive an offer, make sure all enquiries are given top priority. By this I mean, never keep anyone waiting more than a day before you get back to them. As I indicated earlier, "hot prospects" under pressure to buy give no leeway, especially when they're interested in other homes. Real estate agents have heard this reply many times, "I'm sorry, we just put in an offer on another home."

a. HOW TO HANDLE TELEPHONE ENQUIRIES

Over 95% of your enquiries will come from telephone calls. Make sure you possess a telephone answering system; it is especially helpful when you are not home. It decreases your chances of losing the prospect.

1. Don't try to immediately sell the caller

One of the most common problems with the novice seller is the tendency to sell the caller over the phone. Somehow, the vendor's emotional spirits kick in, and then they're trying, very convincingly, to sell the caller, only to have it end up in frustration and wasted time. The first thing good salespeople tell you is: don't try selling the caller over the phone. It is impossible — homes are not like shares listed on the stock exchange.

Answer the caller's initial questions, and then go on the offensive, engaging in dialogue designed primarily to trade questions for questions, in order to get answers you need to assess and qualify the caller. If you want ideas on different approaches, simply call a couple of good salespeople about one of their listings. Before you know it, you'll find that they have more information about you than you have about the property you called about.

2. Do your price and home match callers' expectations?

Ask questions that solicit answers that tell you whether you're in their price range and whether the home conforms to their expectations. For example, an older retired couple won't need a large four-bedroom home. A family with four children won't need a two-bedroom ranch when three bedrooms are barely sufficient. However, if you don't ask those types of questions, you'll never know.

Take time with each caller to discover what you need to know about them, and at the same time extend a genuine interest for their cause. By asking questions and listening carefully to learn what their situation is, the picture becomes much clearer. At that time, if you're satisfied this caller doesn't fit the picture, don't waste any more time because it is unlikely the caller will ever buy your property.

3. Is the caller a "hot prospect?"

Assuming you're in the right price range, and your home reasonably conforms to what the caller needs, try to find out if he or she intends to buy in the near future. Sometimes callers are just looking, prematurely perhaps, with no intention of buying now. Focus on "hot prospects," the ones who intend to buy in the next six months. Don't waste time dealing with all the others. Concentrate on potential purchasers who need to buy within your time table.

4. Does the caller seem financially capable?

Finally, satisfy yourself that the caller is able to qualify for financing in your price range. Only a few potential purchasers think of going to lenders first to determine their financial borrowing power, although on request, lenders do provide this information by pre-qualifying home buyers.

Perhaps the caller has sold his or her home and has recently been transferred to the area and holds a well-paid senior position; that's a good indication of financial capability. Any questions you ask that are designed to discover the person's financial worth should be handled discreetly.

Only after you have answered the caller's basic questions about your home should you proceed with questions designed to obtain the potential caller's financial capability. At this point, enter into a frank exchange similar to the dialogue set out below.

"Have you sold or are you coming from an apartment? (Let's suppose that the caller wants to move from an apartment.) The first time John and I bought our home it was exciting, but frightening too. We didn't know banks would pre-qualify us for a mortgage before we started looking for a home. This time, John and I went to the bank first. Have you ever thought about going to a bank to get pre-qualified? It's really easy. The first thing they ask about is your job situation. John works fill time but I only work part time. How about you people? Your both work — that's great! Banks like that because when two incomes are coming in it's easier to pay mortgage payments. I suppose you'll be applying for a mortgage eventually — won't you? I wish we would win a lotto or something; without those mortgage payments it would be a whole lot easier. John works over at the hat factory on Main

Street and I work part time. What about you and your partner? It sounds like he's some kind of boss or something — is he? Has he worked there for some time?"

By an exchange of information you can make a preliminary qualification of the caller's financial capability to buy. Indirectly you're seeking particular answers by trading information. A caller's unwillingness to disclose answers similar to the above usually indicates that they are merely information seeking and nothing more. When callers are interested, they'll call you again. If the caller seems unwilling, it is best not to pry at this stage.

The preceding test used to qualify callers is important in order to save your time, as well as the caller's. Although you want to get the information, don't handle telephone callers by directing a rapid-fire series of questions — you will come across as abrupt and demanding. Instead, choose questions that are subtle and indirect, but at the same time provide the answers you are looking for. This is easily accomplished, but takes practice. When you're satisfied the caller sounds like a potential buyer, extend an invitation to a private showing.

b. HOW TO CONDUCT A SHOWING

After qualifying the caller, arrange a private showing. Settle on a mutually agreeable date and don't forget to obtain his or her name and phone number. If an emergency comes up, you then have a way of getting in touch in order to cancel. Callers are also less likely to cancel on you, because you know how to reach them. Names and phone numbers are also helpful for contacting callers after the showing, if necessary.

On the day of showing, ask yourself if you have attended to the preparatory work. Your children and animals should be out of sight; arrange for them to visit a relative or neighbor. You don't need unexpected interruptions and prospective purchasers don't need to feel rushed or that they're intruding.

Set up several appointments for the same day. Prospects, knowing others are coming, sometimes get into the competitive spirit. Not wanting anyone to get ahead of them, they're more apt to make a deal right away. It is always easier to arrange several appointments on one day because the whole process of getting ready doesn't have to be repeated as often.

Ask yourself in advance if the landscaping is up to snuff and whether your home is sparkling clean and tidy. Create a pleasing atmosphere, with soft, low music, air fresheners emitting pleasant scents, coffee brewing in the kitchen, and you'll get the effect you need. Turn all lights on, open curtains where additional light is needed or where you want to expose a great view.

Plan the tour methodically in advance; it is always better to save the best for last. In each case the layout of your home should dictate how the tour is charted. Some start at the basement and work their way up; it really doesn't matter as long as you save the best for last.

Conduct a rehearsal in advance to make sure you don't leave anything out.

The moment prospects arrive, greet them with a warm welcome by offering your hand with a cordial introduction. The actual showing shouldn't appear rushed. Avoid drawn out exchanges because prospects need time to concentrate; they are trying to get an impression by mentally placing themselves and their furniture in your home.

Couples communicate verbally back and forth on a frequent basis. Listen carefully for verbal clues and hints. Indirectly, they are telling you how much they are interested in your home. Verbal objections shouldn't be taken seriously, because often they are a positive sign. Beware of the silent ones, especially if they're rushing or seem hurried — the odds are that they won't be back. If a major objection comes up while conducting the tour, avoid getting into a long discussion. Wait until the tour has concluded and address the objection with your solution or comment.

When the prospect still appears interested, it is time to choose your favorite relaxed surrounding. Invite prospects to share their impressions about your home and encourage dialogue while everyone is enjoying a coffee or soft drink.

If you sense a need for prospects to be alone, find some way of excusing yourself in order to give them privacy. After returning, pick up the discussion by asking the potential buyers what they think of your home. If they are still positive, suggest preparing an offer in writing: this is when you'll really know. If they show a positive reaction, introduce your offer to purchase agreement by telling them the form contains a clause requiring their lawyer's approval before it becomes binding. This should relieve any tension prospective buyers have; it lets them know they aren't about to jump overboard without a safety vest. Whenthe deal is a go, then you have the tools to achieve your goal of preparing an agreement of purchase and sale.

Remember, when it comes down to the final crunch, this is a big psychological step to cross. For no reason, you could experience buyers backing away. They may suggest waiting a day or so. Be patient! You still have their phone number and can make another attempt. Don't forget to follow up. If you're successful, attempt another showing and you'll probably get your offer signed. In the next chapter, I discuss the simple strategies used when negotiating your agreement.

11

APPLY THE SIMPLE SELLING STRATEGIES

Now your persistence, preparation, and patience has begun to pay off. By holding fast against the suggestions of real estate agents, by sticking in there through all the grim moments, the peaks and valleys, you have now reached the stage where you must negotiate the agreement of purchase and sale. Many times you may have thought of taking the sign down, but finally you're face-to-face with a potential purchaser, deciding exactly how to negotiate your first agreement. Truly this is a milestone and you should be commended for it!

If you haven't already pointed it out to this "hot prospect," now is a good time to point out the provision in your agreement for getting their lawyer's signed approval before it becomes binding. This provision is contained in section 7 of the agreement of purchase and sale shown in Sample #6. Point out this protection given to the purchaser, because it takes a tremendous amount of pressure off their minds. In private "for sale" situations especially, the purchaser is naturally cautious and some are bound to think owners haven't the expertise of real estate agents. By providing the protection of having their lawyer sanction the deal, they will undoubtedly feel more comfortable negotiating without fear of being trapped.

When you have a partner involved in the sale, it is important to decide who will conduct the negotiations. Having more than one person representing the vendor is cumbersome and sometimes intimidating to the purchaser. As well, it works to your advantage, especially with contentious issues; you can temporarily defer prospects pending consideration by your partner. For example, suppose the purchaser insists on having the living room drapes that are not supposed to be included in the deal. By simply writing the drapes into the agreement and pointing out that it is subject to your partner's approval, you've effectively deferred the issue. The strategy psychologically weakens the purchaser's future bargaining power, because the purchaser doesn't know for sure if the condition is going to be conceded in his or her favor. Also, with only one person present, you won't send conflicting messages, which most purchasers ably grasp to their advantage.

To be a good negotiator, keep the following points in mind:

(a) Be flexible and always be prepared to leave something on the table.

(b) Give in on some issues to secure an advantage on the big issues.

(c) Never assume purchasers are fair and reasonable.

(d) Approach the negotiation table with enthusiasm; moods and attitudes are contagious. Your mental attitude is one of your greatest assets and it will increase your chance for success.

With those points in mind, you'll succeed in applying the following simple negotiating strategies to achieve your goal: getting purchasers to sign on the dotted line of the agreement of purchase and sale. Refer to Sample #6 in chapter 4 when reading the information below.

a. NEGOTIATING PRICE (section 5)

Price is usually the big issue for most purchasers. If you are prepared to concede to a reduction, be careful as to when and how you go about giving it. Decide in advance how far you are prepared to reduce the price and then assess your opponents. Are they so picky that on every point they're going to be difficult negotiators? Sometimes those purchasers are more concerned with the small issues and don't hassle much over larger issues like price. Before finalizing your price, decide if a temporary deferral pending approval strengthens your bargaining position for negotiating the rest of the issues. All purchasers have different attitudes and priorities; that is why negotiating strategies differ in every case.

b. NEGOTIATING THE DEPOSIT (section 6)

The deposit is a negotiated legal pledge paid in good faith to you at the time of signing. The larger the deposit, the better your chances are of keeping the deal together. Try getting between three to five percent of the purchase price. It is only a rule of thumb; smaller or larger amounts may be negotiated depending on the present circumstances of the potential purchaser. For example, if the purchaser's funds are temporarily tied up, a large deposit at the time of signing may be impossible. In such cases, suggest paying the deposit by installments, a modest amount at the time of signing and a substantial amount later when funds are available.

Prearrange all deposit funds to be paid directly to your lawyer's trust account. That gives purchasers assurance their funds are going to be available at the time of closing.

c. NEGOTIATING THE FINANCING CONDITION (section 8)

Negotiating the financing isn't difficult as long as you and the purchaser decide where the financing funds are coming from. Back in chapter 4, the different financing arrangements were discussed. There are six financing arrangements. The most common financing clause is shown in section 8(i) of the agreement of purchase and sale. In that clause the purchaser arranges his or her financing by a new mortgage with a lender of his or her choice. In the other financing arrangements, the purchaser deals with your lender by taking over your mortgage, assuming under one of five possible arrangements set out as follows:

(a) Where there is a straight assumption (section (8)(ii)(a))

(b) Where the existing mortgage is assumed on the condition the principal amount is increased (section (8)(ii)(b))

(c) Where the existing mortgage is assumed and the principal mortgage amount is decreased (section (8)(ii)(c))

(d) Where the existing mortgage is assumed and additional funds are raised by a second mortgage with a third party lender (section (8)(ii)(d))

(e) Where the existing mortgage is assumed and the additional funds are raised by the vendor taking back a second mortgage (section (8)(ii)(e))

In chapter 4, each arrangement is discussed with explanations showing how to complete the blank spaces for each of the different financing clauses.

d. NEGOTIATING FIXTURES AND CHATTELS (section 9)

Fixtures are understood to be part of the purchase price; they don't have to be listed because they're legally part of your deal. For example, a dining room chandelier cannot be removed unless it is provided as an exclusion in the agreement of purchase and sale. This applies to built-in appliances, attached carpeting, doors, light fixtures, etc.

If you have decided that a fixture, such as a chandelier, is not going to be sold with the house, it is always better to remove it and substitute another in its place before you begin the selling process. It could save you a lot of hassle when you're negotiating the terms of the agreement with the purchaser.

The agreement of purchase and sale provides a space for identifying the fixtures to be excluded from your deal. To ensure your intentions are clear, identify the item as an exclusion in the agreement. A fixture must be left, unless you exclude it in section 9 of the agreement.

Chattels, on the other hand, are not considered part of the purchase deal. To include them, you must list them in the agreement. If it is agreed that specific chattels are part of the purchase price, make sure to identify them properly.

Immediately below the area dealing with fixtures in section 9 of the agreement, a space is provided for listing chattels that are to be left as part of the deal. To avoid tax problems, include chattels as part of the total price rather than appropriating separate values for each. See chapter 4, section **f.**, for a more detailed discussion of fixtures and chattels.

e. NEGOTIATING THE CLOSING DATE (section 10)

Selecting a closing date should be easy because you haven't tied yourself to deadlines. During the preparatory stages you arranged your affairs with the potential purchaser in mind, recognizing the possibility of a time constraint.

Consult a calendar to select a specific closing date, making sure the date doesn't fall on a weekend or holiday, when government offices and banks are usually closed. Anyone choosing one of those days will unfortunately have to agree with the purchaser on another date. Otherwise, the law chooses the last business day immediately before the date that was selected in the agreement. If you are forced to comply with that arbitrary date, it could become costly and inconvenient to you.

113

After successfully negotiating the five selling strategies, simply finalize the agreement by having all those whose names appear as parties shown on the front of the agreement sign as indicated along with a witness. As a safety precaution, have your spouse or partner sign on the agreement releasing all his or her rights or interests. When in doubt, consult your lawyer for assistance.

After the formal signing and acknowledgement, provide copies of this agreement to the purchaser's lawyer, your lawyer, the lending institution(s), and one for you and one for the purchasers. Now, the waiting game starts where you wait to hear from the purchaser's lawyer who will review the agreement, and the mortgage lender who gives the written mortgage approval. For the next 15 to 20 days, you'll be on pins and needles waiting to find out if everything is approved.

In the next chapter, I discuss the procedure for removing the purchaser's conditions and the final steps remaining to conclude the selling process.

12

AFTER SIGNING THE AGREEMENT

Before celebrating your successful sale, there are three more aspects to cover: remove all conditions to the sale agreement by getting the purchasers to sign a waiver form; firm up your alternative accommodation, either by renting or buying; and set a time for the movers to get packing.

Don't be too hasty about taking the property off the market while conditions are outstanding in the sale agreement. Continue selling as before. If an interested purchaser comes forth, tell them you have a conditional offer, and you're prepared to give them first chance if your other deal falls through. Then, if the first agreement for some reason fails to get finalized, you haven't let your hopes down, nor have you lost momentum for selling.

a. REMOVAL OF THE PURCHASER'S CONDITIONS

Remember, two conditions in the agreement of purchase and sale are for the benefit of the purchaser (see sections 7 and 8 in Sample #6). The first condition gives the purchaser's lawyer a right to object and cancel the sale agreement. This is only achieved by the lawyer forwarding a letter directly to you within seven days of the acceptance date. This condition is worded so that if you don't receive a reply from the purchaser's lawyer in the time prescribed, the condition automatically is waived, and you can assume everything is satisfactory. But if you receive a letter of objection, immediately get in touch with the purchaser to find out what the

115

problem is. If the purchaser really wants out of the deal, simply close the matter and get on with your selling program.

However, in many cases, the problem is solvable by an amendment to the agreement. If that is the case, suggest that the purchaser's lawyer draft the changes. Afterwards, take the amendment to your lawyer for examination and review. If everything is in order, sign it and send it back to the purchaser and his or her lawyer. Wait until you receive a signed copy from the purchaser.

If the waiver form fails to get signed in time, the deal automatically ends, unless an extension of more time is given in writing before the expiry date. However, if you are confronted with this situation, let the agreement come to an end instead of giving a written extension allowing the purchaser more time for getting the financing approval. Give only your verbal understanding to allow a few more days to get financing, on the condition that thereafter you're reserving your right to entertain new offers from other interested parties. If the purchaser obtains mortgage approval later on, you can still legally revive the agreement through a waiver and acknowledgement form (see Sample #11) by having all of the parties who signed the original agreement sign this waiver form as well. This way you have more control, because it places urgency on the purchaser to push for an early financing approval from the lender, and at the same time, you haven't lost selling momentum.

b. THE WAIVER FORM

The waiver form is a written pre-printed document used for removing conditions in the agreement of purchase and sale. The typical waiver form is reproduced in Sample #11. In addition to waiving conditions in the sale agreement, the document is used for reviving agreements that lapse when time for removing the financing condition has expired. By having all parties to the original agreement sign this form, the wording revives the whole agreement. The signed waiver form changes the sale agreement from conditional to unconditional binding all the parties. As soon as the waiver form is signed, deliver it immediately to the respective lawyers.

c. FIRMING UP YOUR ALTERNATIVE ACCOMMODATION

Whether you decide to rent or purchase, now is the time to enter into a firm commitment for new accommodation so you have a place to live by the closing date. For renting situations, sign a formal lease and make the arrangements for:

(a) getting keys,

(b) contacting an insurance agent for contents coverage, and

(c) changing over the utility accounts such as water, gas, hydro, cable, and telephone, effective on the closing date.

When purchasing another property, sign a waiver form removing the condition for selling your home and immediately submit a mortgage application form to the lender. If a survey is necessary, order it right away with instructions to have the report forwarded directly to your lawyer when it is available. As soon as the mortgage commitment is received from your lender, sign the waiver form removing the financing condition for your new purchase agreement. Removal of these conditions creates an unconditional and binding deal on everyone.

The lawyer, on receipt of the waiver form removing conditions, knows there is a limited period of time to finalize the deal, so he or she will immediately work on it. At this point, both the sale and the purchase deals are your lawyer's responsibility to ensure that both deals get finalized on the closing date.

117

SAMPLE #11
ACKNOWLEDGMENT AND WAIVER FORM

TO WHOM IT MAY CONCERN

RE: PROPERTY KNOWN AS _____

_____

_____

_____

(Enter the full legal description of the property)

We the undersigned, hereby acknowledge as existing and binding on us an Agreement of Purchase and Sale accepted at _____ _____ , _____ , the_____day of_____19___ .

Accordingly, we waive the financing condition(s) and hereby acknowledge that all conditions are hereby waived save and except the condition set out in section 11 of the Agreement of Purchase and Sale.

WAIVED AT _____ , this _____ day of _____ _____ 19___ .

SIGNED, SEALED, AND DELIVERED IN WITNESS, I HAVE SET MY HAND AND SEAL

in the presence of:

_____   _____

Witness   *Purchaser*

_____   _____

_____   _____

Witness   *Vendor*

_____   _____

We hereby acknowledge receipt of this waiver on _____ day of _____ 19___ .

d. ARRANGING FOR MOVERS AND FINAL DETAILS

Hire a moving company well in advance to guarantee availability on the closing day. A few days prior to completion, contact the utility companies with instructions to read the meters and adjust accounts as of the date you are moving. Cancel and rearrange insurance coverage with your property insurance agent. Then start packing and cleaning to get an early head start on the final day.

You've now concluded the list of arrangements needed to make an orderly transfer on closing day. After you are moved into your new home, reflect on this new experience and the knowledge you've acquired by conducting your own private sale. Of course, take part of the commission savings to do something truly rewarding for all your hard work. You deserve it!

GLOSSARY

AGENCY

The relationship between an agent, also known as a broker, and the real estate owner

AGENT

A person authorized by the owner to conduct business transactions with potential purchasers

AGREEMENT OF PURCHASE AND SALE

The written contract between the purchaser and the vendor for the sale of property

AMORTIZATION PERIOD

The amount of time it takes to gradually pay back the entire mortgage amount

APPRAISAL REPORT

A written document containing an estimate of value as of a specified date with supporting analysis and material data

APPRAISER

A person with special qualifications for giving an estimate of value on property

APPURTENANCE

Something outside of the real property itself, but belongs to the land and is joined to it adding more enjoyment to the land such as a right-of-way over the adjoining owner's land

ASSESSED VALUE

The value attributable to real estate shown on the municipal tax rolls for taxation purposes

ASSUMPTION OF MORTGAGE

Where the purchaser assumes liability for an existing mortgage against the vendor's property and becomes personally liable for payment of the mortgage debt

CLOSING

The date the purchaser and vendor agree to complete the transfer of title

COMMISSION

The remuneration paid to an agent on the sale of property usually based on a percentage of the selling price

CONVEYANCE

The transfer of an interest in property usually from the vendor to the purchaser

DATE OF COMPLETION (CLOSING DATE)

The date in the agreement of purchase and sale when the purchaser delivers money and or other security in exchange for the vendor delivering a properly executed deed or transfer in a form acceptable for registration, keys, and vacant possession of the property (unless otherwise agreed)

DEPOSIT

Payment of money or other valuable consideration given by the purchaser as a pledge for good faith to fulfill the contract

DOWN PAYMENT

The amount of money the purchaser has to put towards the purchase price after satisfying all of the costs associated with purchasing the property (apart from mortgages arranged)

DUE DATE

This refers to the date when mortgages must be either paid in full or another term negotiated through a renewal agreement

EASEMENT

A right enjoyed by one land owner over all or part of an adjoining owner's land

ENCUMBRANCE

An outstanding lien, claim, or charge registered by a person against the property owned by another

EQUITY

The owner's net value left after payment of all mortgages, liens, and claims

LEGAL DESCRIPTION

A written description definitely describing the property and acceptable for registration

LISTING AGREEMENT

A written document where the property owner agrees to remunerate an agent (broker) for successfully marketing the owner's property

MARKET PRICE

The amount actually paid or to be paid for the sale of the property

MARKET VALUE

The probable price a property should bring in a competitive and open market under conditions of a fair sale

MORE OR LESS

A vague term used in some agreements for sale to indicate the quantity or extent of the owner's property

MORTGAGE

A conveyance of a property right to a lender or creditor as security for payment of a debt

MORTGAGEE

The person or company who receives the property interest as security for payment of the debt

MORTGAGOR

The owner who gives the property interest to a lender or creditor as security for payment of the debt

MULTIPLE LISTING SERVICE

The distribution of listings by a real estate board to all of its participating members. The vendor usually pays a higher commission rate for this service

NULL AND VOID

A phrase used in agreements to signify that certain actions constitute the agreement as having no validity or legal effect

PROPERTY LINES

The borders of an owner's property that are accurately defined on a survey

RIGHT OF WAY

The right of one property owner to pass over the lands of another property owner which is established by an easement or a licence agreement

TERM

This refers to the space of time mortgage funds are borrowed, on the expiry date the debt obligation is either paid in full or a new term negotiated

TIME IS OF THE ESSENCE

A phrase used in an agreement of purchase and sale calling for punctual performance on stated dates with failure to comply resulting in a potential breach of contract unless otherwise agreed in writing

TITLE

Generally means the outward evidence of a person's right to the possession of the property

TRANSFER

To convey property from one person to another person

VENDOR

The person who is selling the property

WAIVER FORM

A document used to waive conditions set out in an agreement of purchase and sale to create an unconditional legal binding agreement

WITNESS

A person subscribing his or her name for the purpose of attesting to a document's authenticity and proving he or she saw the parties place their signatures on the document